LIONPROOF:

KEEPING YOUR CHILDREN FROM THE CLAWS OF THE DEVIL

Based on exclusive interviews with the young people who survived!

By Lisa B. Raub

Eagle Heights Publications
Raeford, NC

Eagle Heights Publications, NC

Lionproof: Keeping Your Children from the Claws of the Devil

Copyright © 2014 by Kevin and Lisa Raub

ISBN:978-0-9892908-0-7

LCCN: 2013937991

Visit www.TheCourageousJourney.com or www.EW-MM.org for more information on other products by Eagle Heights Publications

Requests for information should be addressed to: Eagle Heights Publications, PO Box 443, Raeford, NC 28376 USA

Cover design, interior design and layout by Indie Designz

Printed in the United States of America

eagle heights
PUBLICATIONS

This book is lovingly dedicated to my children:

Kathryn, Jonathan, Stephen, Sharon,

Lydia, Johanna, & Jason

with their dear spouses and beautiful children!

May you raise godly generations that will reach many for the Savior!

TABLE OF CONTENTS:

INTRODUCTION:

I believe that these pages hold life-changing truths for future generations. By taking the Word of God seriously and focusing our attention on raising a godly generation, we have the keys to thwarting Satan's insidious attacks. With the backing of many Christian parents that have gone on before and successfully raised godly young people, we will see that we too can do it. Best of all, through their encouragement and shining example, we will find strength to deal with our own situations.

For me, this study has been sometimes surprising, many times shocking, and through time, life-altering. It has been a challenge and a blessing, an encouragement and a conviction. Each interview has impacted my life immensely, and I think their stories can change yours as well.

Most of all, I believe you will find encouragement to not settle for anything less than the best, while depending on a gracious and kind God. My prayer is that everyone reading this book will find the support they need to raise a godly generation.

It has been done.
It can be done.
It *must* be done.

. . . to God be the glory!

Author's Note: Throughout this book the names have been changed to protect those who have been gracious enough to share their stories.

ACKNOWLEDGEMENTS:

So many people have had a hand in the publication of this book, that it's hard to thank them all...but I'll try! My husband Kevin has been a huge supporter of this project from the beginning, setting up interview appointments, sitting in some interviews with me, and generally putting up with about 5 years of discussion of this subject. In spite of it all, he still loves me!

Of course, my four younger children who still live at home have also had to put up with my many interviews, and the three married ones have endured several years' worth of discussion! Their support and love for me through this has been a great encouragement. Two comments especially stand out in my mind. Afraid I was spending too much time at the keyboard, I asked one of my older sons if he thought I spent too much time writing. He looked at me, puzzled, and asked, "You write?" And another one of my kids remarked as I was preparing this book for printing, "You know, I've never even looked at your book. I don't even know what it's about." These responses keep me laughing and show me that they have not felt slighted by the amount of time taken to write. That in itself is huge to me.

Many dear people have, either under duress or voluntarily, proofread this, and I thank them for all their help! Judy Truax supplied much valuable insight, while my friend Tawn Lowell also kindly gave very good advice. My two daughters, Kathryn (Raub) Siegwart and Sharon Raub, AKA "The Grammar Gestapo" (why did I decide to home school??) were brutal, but incredibly helpful. They performed the most difficult task of correcting the teacher's work! Or maybe they enjoyed a little bit of "red pen revenge!"

And I could never forget the dozens of people who I was able to interview. You know who you are! Thank you sooooo much for taking the time to give us your priceless stories! May God wonderfully bless you, and use you!

Finally, I thank my Lord, for saving my soul, and for giving me the whole idea for this book and granting me the persistence to see it through. He is so good!!

PART 1

The Tragedy
&
The Survivors

CHAPTER 1:
WITNESS THE TRAGEDY

"Three out of every five (59%) young Christians disconnect either permanently or for an extended period of time from church life after age 15."[1]

It was the journey of a lifetime, and the young man was enjoying his new situation to the fullest. Taking a job as a water-bearer for the new bridge-building project in Africa was just the thing to get him away from the rigid rules of home, make some good money, and have a little excitement.

Unfortunately, his adventure quickly turned morbid.

The stillness of night was shattered by the water-bearer's screams. "Let go! Let go!" he shrieked into the darkness. His tent-mates trembled as they listened helplessly to the awful commotion. The young man's strangled cries mingled with growling and snorting as he tried vainly to fight off his attacker. Though it seemed like hours, it was only a few seconds till he was gone—torn from his peaceful bed by the enormous creature, which bounded out of the tent with its prey.

His comrades listened as the growling trailed off into the jungle, and soon all was silent. Regaining their senses, they scrambled to Colonel Patterson's tent, barging through the opening to tell their gruesome tale. "Simba! Simba!" they shrieked, eyes wide with terror. ("Lion! Lion!") Colonel Patterson quickly ran to the small canvas hut, and looked around. His keen eyes took in the entire scene, and all too soon it became evident to him what had happened to the young man.

"Too bad he was right by the door," he remarked grimly, gesturing to the marks on the ground. The colonel's eyes followed the furrows dug by the young man's heels as he was dragged away. "Looks like the lion took him that way- off into the jungle."

The year was 1898. Deep in the jungles of Kenya, British Lieutenant Colonel John Patterson had recently arrived from India to take charge of the building of a bridge across the Tsavo River. However, within a short time, the work had been was interrupted in a most horrifying manner.

Two of the coolies, Indian workers employed in the bridge building project, mysteriously disappeared. Patterson thought perhaps they had fallen victim to foul play on the part of their fellow workers, especially since the two men had a small savings. The coolies, however, knew differently. They insisted that the workers had been carried off and devoured by a man-eating lion.

It wasn't long until Patterson learned they were right. About three weeks after his arrival, he was informed that one of the jemedars—a fine, strapping young water-bearer—had been caught during the night, dragged out of his tent, and eaten. At the tent, Patterson found heel marks and a trail of blood which led him to a gory scene of death.

Following the blood-spattered furrows was bad enough, but the sight that greeted him in the jungle was chilling. Rounding a bend in the trail, the hardened colonel came to a halt and gasped in shock. In silence, he and his team took in the ghastly scene. Fragments of bones and flesh were strewn about, accentuated by massive claw marks in the dirt.

"Look there," he pointed. It was the man's head, still intact, with a fixed, terrified gaze. Patterson quickly looked away and sighed, then walked around to examine the tracks. "I think, from the two different sizes of tracks, that we're dealing with not only one lion, but two!" He indicated the scuffle marks that seemed to be everywhere. "Apparently, there was a fight for the body."

The night had begun with a young man with high hopes, dreams, and a life of adventure ahead of him—but it ended in horrific tragedy.

The Predator is on the move.

Just as these man-eating lions targeted individuals for their meals, Satan has targeted our children. 1 Peter 5:8 states, "Your adversary the devil, as a roaring lion, walketh about, seeking whom he may devour." Whether we are aware of it or not, there is a great battle being fought in the world—and souls are the objective. Satan has deceived an unbelievable number of our second generation, telling them that Christianity is simply not worth it. Many others have been paralyzed for one reason or another, rendering them numb and ineffective in the service of the Lord. It is a spiritual epidemic sweeping our nation, taking with it our most precious possession: our children. They are streaming out of our church doors by the thousands, their arms tightly linked with the world, walking lock-step (whether they realize it or not) with the Predator.

HERE'S THE TYPICAL CARNAGE WE WITNESS TODAY:

One lady of my acquaintance, who is normally quite cheerful, grew very sober as she spoke of her older brother. "We were raised in a good Christian home, but as soon as he got out of the house, he stopped going to church," Dianne said sadly. "He's older than I am, and hasn't been to church in about 27 years. He's just not at all interested in the things of God, and my parents wonder if he was ever really saved. The sad part is the effect this has had on his children. His family is in shambles; his marriage is virtually nonexistent and his kids are heavily involved with drinking and drugs."She sighed, and I realized that this lady and her brother were raised in the same home, but are philosophically worlds apart now.

It is not uncommon for Christian young people to "jump ship" at age eighteen, leaving people scratching their heads and saying, "I wonder what happened?" It is almost like they are being stolen right from their comfortable tents, dragged away and eaten! There seems to be no predictability—no rhythm, no pattern—to the attack of the Devil, and he shows no regard to the person's station or position in life. Even pastors', deacons', and missionaries' children have fallen by the wayside at alarming rates. (And some would say *especially* those children!) It is an epidemic that is sweeping through our churches.

Check out these statistics from The Barna Group—an evangelical research organization which examines the cultural pulse of modern Christianity:

> In fact, the most potent data regarding disengagement is that a majority of twenty-somethings—61% of today's young adults—had been churched at one point during their teen years but they are now

spiritually disengaged (i.e., not actively attending church, reading the Bible, or praying). Only one-fifth of twenty-somethings (20%) have maintained a level of spiritual activity consistent with their high school experiences. Another one-fifth of teens (19%) were never significantly reached by a Christian community of faith during their teens and have remained disconnected from the Christian faith.

For most adults, this pattern of disengagement is not merely a temporary phase in which they test the boundaries of independence, but is one that continues deeper into adulthood, with those in their thirties also less likely than older adults to be religiously active. Even the traditional impulse of parenthood—when people's desire to supply spiritual guidance for their children pulls them back to church—is weakening. The new research pointed out that just one-third of twenty-somethings who are parents regularly take their children to church , compared with two-fifths of parents in their thirties and half of parents who are 40-years-old or more.[2]

This study indicates what I have been noticing in churches all across the country: that many young people are turning their back on church, never to return.

Here's another terrifying statistic. *The Christian Post* reported in January of, 2006:

Researchers found between 69-94 percent of Christian youths forsake their faith after leaving high school. The Barna Group reported 64 percent loss after college graduation. The Assemblies of God conducted a 10-year study and found 75 percent loss of their students within one year of high school graduation, while the Southern Baptists found that number to be even higher at 88 percent loss. And Josh McDowell Ministries reports 94 percent fallout within two years of high school graduation.[3]

Though these statistics are quite alarming to me, but my experience tells me they are accurate. I personally know of many families who have been affected. In fact, several of my own children's friends have simply run away from their homes for all sorts of reasons. The situation is quite difficult on the parents, the brothers and sisters, and especially to the young person themselves. Starting life on the run is quite a rough beginning.

Some are concerned.

Thankfully, there are some who are investigating this "slaughter from another world". Some are asking very important questions, seeking to understand why so many of our second generation are going astray. There have been a number of books written to help us understand some of the reasons why our young people are leaving our churches in droves. Already Gone, by Ken Ham, and Jumping Ship, by Michael Pearl are just two of the excellent books that have been written to address this subject. While I do not endorse everything these men believe, I think their research on the church and family is very well done, and their ideas are superb.

Why is it so important that we protect our families from the ravages of Satan? Why must we preserve the second generation? Here are just a few of the reasons:

- Without second generation Christians, there would be fewer workers to win others.

- Losing the second generation means that the foundation for Christianity must be laid again and again, instead of building on that of the previous generation.

- Second generation Christian "deserters" create a poor testimony for Christian homes, in effect stating, "Christianity is toxic."

- The vacuum caused by those who leave creates a tremendous negative impact on those who remain, causing anything from guilt to doubt in real Bible Christianity.

Losing our second generation is a very serious thing. We as parents need to figure out what's going on, and *do* something about it!

In 1898, Lieutenant Colonel Patterson realized something had to be done to stop the savage man-eaters of Tsavo. He also understood that the job was his, and no one else's. Armed with incredible bravery, knowledge of the jungle, and a grim determination to do whatever was necessary, he picked up his weapons and ammunition and began what was to be the most important hunt of his life. The future of his workers, and even the entire future of the bridge, hung in the balance.

For Patterson, life would never be the same. It was either hunt, or be hunted. And for us as Christians, it is time to turn around the maniacal stalking of Satan. For us, there can be no choice; we must hunt, or be hunted. We must thwart his schemes by a proactive plan for our families, or else allow our children to be pulled out right from their "safe"Christian homes and be devoured by the Devil. It is time to *do* something, and what better plan than the one that has worked through the ages?

CHAPTER 2:
MEET THE SURVIVORS

Discovering Their Stories

Either what woman having ten pieces of silver, if she lose one piece, doth not light a candle, and sweep the house, and seek diligently till she find it? (Luke 15:8)

Having seven children of my own, some of whom are already grown and serving the Lord themselves, I am intensely interested in the subject of retaining the next generation. I've watched the enemy stalk them! Some of my close acquaintances have had child after child turn 18 and then turn away from God and live completely differently than the way they were raised. I also know families who have had young person after young person turn eighteen and continue on the path of serving the Lord. Throughout the 25 years that my family has been in ministry, I have had people ask my advice on godly child-rearing, and even suggest that I write my own book on training children.

So I began working on a parenting book of my own. About 75 pages into it, it dawned on me that I was merely writing my personal—therefore fallible—opinion! I was a bit discouraged by that thought, but soon the Lord gave me a new idea: *Wouldn't it be wonderful to talk to parents who have raised their children for God* successfully, *to find out what they did? After all, I may have three children out of the nest, but I'm not done yet. Yes,* I thought, someone *needs to do that, and write a book about it!*

In what seemed like a few short seconds God made it clear to me: *I* was in a perfect position to ask the questions. *I* was to be the one to do the research.

And *I* was to be the one to write the book.

The more I tried to talk myself (and God) out of it, the more I realized that God has given me unusual opportunities to make the contacts, ask the questions, look for similarities in the answers, and to write out my findings. Having been on the road for most of the past seventeen years, I have met *thousands* of people. I have had the opportunity to talk to them, find out about their lives, and learn about their families. As we minister in different churches, I spend time with hundreds of people, and know them well enough to ask some very important, yet personal, questions.

I became possessed with a singular thought: instead of asking the question, "Why do many young people leave?" I want to know "*Why do some stay?*" Just as there is often a reason why many young people turn away from God, there must be some reason why some *choose* to serve the Lord. The question is not, "What do many do wrong?" but "*What do some do right?*"

It's easy to read up on what is going *wrong*, but have you ever thought about what is going *right*? It is like the two posts of a battery. If you didn't have the negative *and* the positive connections, there would be no flow of power. No spark—no start, no results. And what better way to find out what I need to do RIGHT as a parent, than to look at the many successful role models here in this world today? Nothing compares to the wit and knowledge of another parent who has successfully navigated the confusing seas of child training.

At first, I began talking to first-generation Christians, whom I know have godly adult children who love the Lord and are active in church. But that just wasn't...*conclusive.* One dear older lady, a retired home educator whose two children are serving God, looked at me with a puzzled expression. When I asked how she raised such godly young people, she hesitated. "Well, I don't know . . . pray??" Then she decided, "I guess God did it!" I left the conversation with even *more* questions. It's very true; God *did* work in their family and help them raise another generation of godly Christians, but I wondered *how* God worked in their lives. I wanted to know how they did it.

Then I began talking to their adult children: the ones who are now happily serving God because of the influence of their parents. Each of the people in my interviews made his *own* decision to follow God, independent of his parents. Unlike the parents, who may not know exactly what they did right, these young people *know* why they are serving God. And, they also know why many of their peers are *not* serving the Lord today!

To this end, I formulated a survey designed to discover parenting practices, philosophies, actions, and attitudes —as seen from the eyes of the young people themselves. These are the godly Christians who have outlasted the insidious attacks of Satan on their families. Their parents have thwarted the fiery darts of the world, the flesh, and the Devil to help make their children Lionproof, retaining them for God. They have pressed on through the battles, kept the faith, and passed the torch. The faithful parents are the Defenders, and the children are the Survivors. And now, the Survivors speak out on *what their parents did right*!

The Most Sincere and Godly People I've Ever Met

As I began interviewing, I was privileged to talk to some of the finest people in the United States. I talked to many second, third and fourth- generation Christians and even a few fifth or sixth generation! These last were the most interesting to me, because of how their parents' faith had been passed down through so many years.

When I first began searching, I was pleasantly surprised to find more of them than I originally thought. Since they are amongst us, quietly working beside us in the Lord's work, we often do not realize they are there. Yet often they are the ones pushing forward the work of God. They are manning our church nurseries, passing out church flyers, leading the singing or filling the choir. Faithfully they work and pray, following God and raising their children for Him just as their parents did.

Some are more visible. Some are preaching the Word of the Lord, resounding from our pulpits the inerrant Word of God. Some are Christian school teachers, pointing their students to the Lord who made them. Some are professors in our Bible colleges, preparing the next generation for service to our Savior. Because of the work of these second-generation Christians,

Christianity goes on . . . and on . . . and on . . . and the torch is passed to the next generation.

I began to wonder if perhaps there are certain concepts and philosophies that produce happy, godly young people, no matter their personality, locality, background, or the age of their parents. So I began looking for these things during my interviews. My goal was to find similar traits or qualities in the way each person was raised. As they are completely diverse from each other, finding similar answers would be very crucial. If several people gave the same answer to a question, then I would know that that point had more validity to it. If almost everyone gave the same answer, then I could be sure I hit on a *key* point. And so I began asking questions.

Those I interviewed ranged from twenty-three years old to seventy-nine years old, with an average age of thirty-nine. I talked to people in Texas, California, Oregon, Washington, Louisiana, Florida, Pennsylvania, Indiana, Michigan, North Carolina, South Carolina, Kansas, Georgia, Mississippi, and Idaho. As of this writing, I've spoken with dozens of people, an equal number of men and women.

My criteria for these interviews were multi-faceted. First, the second-generation individual must be saved. By this, I mean that they have had a definite born-again experience, bringing about a positive change in their life. They must believe in salvation by grace through faith.

Another prerequisite that I looked for is that the individual is actively serving God in a Bible-preaching church. These godly folks whose stories you will hear are not your average Sunday morning crowd; they are the very backbone of the ministry, serving God any way they can. I believe firmly that a truly godly second-generation Christian WILL be involved, in whatever way, in the work of the Lord.

Vastly important to me in demonstrating that they are true Survivors is whether the person is active in evangelism. Evangelism must take place both passively, through a godly lifestyle, as well as actively, by taking initiative and presenting the gospel to others verbally or through written media. To me, a Christian who is building upon the foundation of godly parents should not only *live a godly life*, but they must also have a desire to turn others to the Savior, as well.

I also looked for people that are striving to bring their own children up in the nurture and admonition of the Lord. It has been said that the most convincing evidence is not found in the second generation themselves, but in whether or not the second generation is training up their children in the way of the Lord. These, then, are folks who have taken the concept of passing on the torch of the Gospel seriously, and are trying to teach their own children to serve God as well.

Field-Tested, Mother-Approved!

Through these interviews, I have been able to discern patterns of successful parenting practices. I have taken these patterns and outlined them, then used the exact words of the second (or third, etc.) generation Christian to explain the patterns, just as I received them. The result is that the principles in this book are not just theories or the opinions of an author conjuring up good-sounding, but untested material. Rather, they have been proven by *generation after generation* of Christians who have raised their young people to love and live for God.

Also, these principles are not unattainable ideals that can only be reached by the perfect parent; they are truths that have been used very effectively by imperfect people living in an imperfect world--many times even in difficult situations. Some of these principles have confirmed things I already knew, while others have completely changed my life. I believe that if we learn from what these young people have told us, we can have an excellent grasp on how to raise a *godly* generation. May we be willing to make the changes necessary to reach that goal.

Points to Remember:
There are a few things to keep in mind while reading this book:

1. Though God blesses obedience, parenting is not a formula. God is not in man's box. He is not a genie that will come out of the bottle and give us everything we want if we rub it the right way. Parenting is a process of learning the sweet lesson of obeying God and listening to His Spirit through every decision and stage of life.

2. There will be as many shades of varying parenting practices as there are personalities. Some of the parents discussed in this book dealt with their wayward children subtly, while some reacted more strenuously. There may be, then, perhaps no one way to deal with all children. God created us as individuals!

3. The study is not truly objective, nor can it be. Due to the nature of the process of choosing interviewees, it is a subjective study, based on my perception of the individuals' desire to serve God. I can say without a doubt that I believe wholeheartedly that the people I have talked to are as true and sincere as any human beings on the planet, and so I have no reservation to recommend them as splendid examples of Bible-believing Christianity. So it is not devoid of my opinion. However, I think there are enough examples of godly parenting to create undeniable evidence for the points discussed.

4. My desire is to be a *blessing* to those seeking to train their children for God, not to discourage someone. If someone reading this has already lost some (or all) of their children to the world, please understand that I do not intend to put all of the responsibility for a child's decisions on the shoulders of the parents. There are some parents that are reaping what they have sown, but that is not always the case. One of the folks I interviewed, Clare, told me this story:

> My dad, a pastor, and my mom have blamed themselves for years for my wayward brother's behavior. As a young man, he chose to give himself over to the world, and of course is reaping the repercussions now that he's older. Throughout the years, my parents have asked themselves—and God—over and over, "What did we do wrong with our son? How could we have done a better job raising him?" Blaming themselves for his behavior, they grieved for years. One day, they decided to just come out and ask him the question that had been plaguing them. Heartbroken, they came to him and asked, "What could we have done to help you love and serve the Lord? What did we do wrong?"
>
> After a short pause, he cleared his throat and looked deeply into their eyes. "You guys are the best parents in the world, and always have been. It was a choice *I decided* to make. You didn't do anything wrong." My mom and dad finally found the peace they so

desperately needed, because they understood that, in the end, it was <u>his choice</u>.

Perhaps you are grieving, like those dear parents. Please understand that there may have been nothing you could have done differently; some young people simply choose to go astray.

If, however, the Lord uses some of these words to gently reveal something to you, do what you must: confess the sin and forsake it . . . for the sake of your children; for your grandchildren. The Lord is plenteous in mercy and His loving-kindness is infinite!

How To Use This Book

Before each chapter, there are some Thought Questions, designed to jump-start your brain before you actually get into the material. Each chapter has a case study: the story of someone who may have a situation similar to yours, or who may be a second-generation Christian in a home like your own. Material derived from the interviewees themselves comprises the balance of the chapter. Then, at the chapter's end, you will find a section titled, "Preparing *Your* Defense," in which you get the opportunity to take what you've learned and apply it to your own life and family. There is an assignment, sometimes two, at the very end. Take your time as you go through these important steps; it is the meditation on the Scriptural principles that will bring about the necessary changes.

In this book, we will examine the most important attitudes of those who have already raised godly young people, and will tell the stories of how they dealt with some difficulties. We will get into the challenges of raising teenagers for God, and also into one of the things I think is most exciting: the keys to passing on godly values. We will explore the imperfections of successful parents, and show how they dealt with anger and irritation in their lives. We will also discuss the tenuous period of launching young people into the world, and give key thoughts regarding the best ways to "let go."

Toward the end of the book, there is a section that deals with the responses of those who I call "Exceptions." In other words, they do not fit into the normal pattern for those raised in Christian homes, and yet they are serving God. A few folks had grown up in dysfunctional homes, divorce situations, or even sexual abuse situations. But I feel that these exceptions are as valuable as the norms, since they show us that, even through extreme difficulties, a young person can still serve God effectively. And, although it is no excuse for a parent to be involved in these detrimental activities, we can see that God can work miracles in spite of our shortcomings.

Most of all, I believe you will find encouragement to not settle for anything less than the best. My prayer is that everyone reading this will find the support they need to raise a godly generation.

PART TWO

YOUR DEFENSIVE FOCUS

What you ARE

THOUGHT QUESTIONS for Chapter 3

1. What, in your opinion, is the most important quality a successful parent must have?

2. Do you think it is more important to *do the right thing* or to *have the right attitude?* How can we do both?

3. How is faith increased? Can the examples of others increase our faith?

CHAPTER 3:
THE SURVIVORS SPEAK OUT—
THE PRIMARY KEY TO SUCCESS

~Some peoples' Christianity is one hundred miles wide, but only a fraction of an inch deep.~author unknown

*"Let love be **without dissimulation**[hypocrisy]. Abhor that which is evil; cleave to that which is good." (Romans 12:9)*

*"Now therefore fear the LORD, and serve him **in sincerity and in truth**: and put away the gods which your fathers served on the other side of the flood, and in Egypt; and serve ye the LORD." (Joshua 24:14)*

Have you ever felt like a failure at raising your children? Have you ever felt that there was no way your kids could turn out for God? Perhaps you, like me, have looked at other parents who seem better than you and watched as *their* children grow sour on God and blow out into the world, and thought to yourself, "If *these* parents lost their own children, how could *I* possibly train *my* children to love and serve the Lord?"

How can I Lionproof my own children—strengthen their faith so that they are kept from the claws of the Devil? Can it even be done?

Satan is always prowling around, looking for his next meal, and children are his favorite morsels. However, generations of Christians have successfully raised their young people to serve the Lord—people just like you and me. Folks with trials, financial difficulties, and physical troubles have all effectively navigated the difficulties of our current godless culture to raise a generation of young people who love God. They are The Survivors, and here is their story.

Their parents began Lionproofing their children by first **building a solid foundation.**

What's the foundation of the home? The Christian home's foundation begins *before* two become one; it begins with each individual before they even approach the marriage altar. It begins with each individual's relationship with God.

While sitting at a church fellowship recently, I talked with an older lady named Karen. She was telling me about her husband's and her fiftieth wedding anniversary they celebrated earlier in the year, and how the whole family got together. "We only have two children. Sarah," she pointed to the pastor's wife, who was sitting at another table at the church fellowship, "and Joe, who lives in Oklahoma. Of course, they are both active in church, and the Lord has given them nine children between the two of them. It's such a blessing how they are training their children to serve the Lord. God's been so good to me!" she brushed a tear from her eye.

"But I was raised in a dysfunctional family. My mother had no time for God, and disliked the fact that I sometimes went to church. I hate to say it, but she and my father were foul-mouthed and mean. I was so thankful that two of my aunts took an interest in me, and took me to Vacation Bible School every year, and to church sometimes. I guess it was because of their influence that I trusted Christ as my Savior, and then started going to church faithfully, even though my family didn't like it. I was only twelve when I began going to a Bible-preaching church by myself."

Karen continued her story. "The Lord had a special plan for my husband and me. We met at a gas station, and were married three weeks later," she told me with a twinkle in her eye. My jaw must have dropped, because she quipped, "Did it work?" Karen laughed and pointed to her smiling husband of 50 years, "Here's proof!"

"Seriously, though, I believe God put my husband and me together for the purpose of raising children that will live for Him. We made plenty of mistakes, raising our children," she continued. "But I tried my best to apologize, too. I know also that we were all involved in church as a family. As a matter of fact, when Joe moved away from home, he continued his work with the Kids' Bible Club at church. It's something he still does, even now that he's in his fifties!"

The primary key to Karen's success is just what was echoed by many other second-generation Christians as being the most important thing that kept them in the faith. What was it? I'm so glad you asked!

First:

It's Not What Most People Think!

When the Barna Group did a study and asked Christian parents what qualities they felt good parents should have, the results were quite disappointing.

Walking quietly through the jungle, the massive maneless lion felt the gnawing pain of hunger. He licked his chops as he began trotting toward the camp where the coolies lay sleeping. Every muscle in his body moved together to create a fluid motion which would have been almost beautiful, had it not been for his chilling errand.

Soon, he could sense that the camp was not far ahead of him, and he quietly stalked toward the clearing. Within seconds, he spied what he wanted: a young coolie walking toward his tent, completely unaware of the danger he was in. He was a marked man, and he didn't even know it.

Now was not the time for the attack. Though it was twilight, the huge cat would wait until total darkness . . . until it was his time. Flicking his tail ever so slightly, his cold eyes narrowed as he watched his intended prey go into the tent. It mattered little that there was a canvas shield around his meal. The beast could and would easily tear through any barrier to get his selected food. His keen ears heard the young man prepare for bed, and he marked the place where the coolie lay down.

Darkness was coming. Soon he would eat.

"You might expect that parents who are born again Christians would take a different approach to raising their children than did parents who have not committed their life to Christ—but that was rarely the case," Barna explained. "For instance, we found that **the qualities born again parents say an effective parent must possess, the outcomes they hope to facilitate in the lives of their children, and the media monitoring process in the household was indistinguishable from the approach taken by parents who are not born again."**[4](emphasis mine)

Think about it: what the study revealed is that your average born-again parent approaches parenting in exactly the same way as those parents who don't care at all about God. Let it not be said of us that our parenting process is just like the average.

The same study reveals that:

> **"Only three out of ten born again parents included the salvation of their child in the list of critical parental emphases,"** he noted. "Parents cannot force or ensure that their kids become followers of Christ. **But for that emphasis to not be on the radar screen of most Christian parents is a significant reason why most Americans never embrace Jesus Christ as their Savior.** We know that parents still have a huge influence on the choices their children make, and we also know that most people either accept Christ when they are young or not at all. The fact that most Christian parents overlook this critical responsibility is one of the biggest challenges to the Christian Church." (emphasis mine)

If we have the same attitudes toward parenting that the lost world has, we should not be at all surprised when our outcomes are no different than theirs. The goal should not be to raise *good* kids, but to raise *godly* kids, and that can't happen if they don't have a relationship with God. Unfortunately, the evidence shows that your average Christian parent does not even consider the salvation of their children to be on their list of priorities!

My respondents, however, know differently. They recognize that the qualities of successful parents must be different than the world. Their goals will be different, and the media monitoring process will be different. Our guiding principles, God helping us, must be based on the Word of God.

What is the most important characteristic of a godly parent who successfully raises godly children? Some may think that in order to raise godly children, we need to be perfect parents. Is it truly perfection that is required? Must we be virtually sinless, spotless, and infinitely patient? What really *is* the most important characteristic in godly parenting?

The Most Important Quality of a Successful parent

Throughout the generations, there is one time-and-culture tested quality that has been effective in passing on the Gospel torch. It's not rocket science; it is very basic. It's also not just a theory; it's a principle that has been successful over the years. Second-generation Christians know the answer.

In almost every one of my interviews, the same characteristic popped up. I simply asked the question, "Is there anything your parents did or did not do that pointed you in the direction of serving God?" **I wanted to ask an open question so that the individual spoke from his own thoughts, rather than being put into a multiple-choice mold.** Most of the respondents independently volunteered, in their own words and of their own volition, the very same characteristic. To me, this individual repetition is very powerful evidence that this trait is one of the most—if not truly *the* very most—important attribute that a godly parent must possess, in order to raise godly children.

So what is this single, crucial quality? I'll let one of my respondents answer. Though Julia is almost 50, she is strikingly beautiful, thoughtful, and almost painfully candid. I asked, "Is there anything that your parents did or did not do that pointed you in the direction of serving God?" The middle-aged pastor's wife looked gazed thoughtfully for a moment before answering. Then, looking straight at me, she leaned forward and smiled. "My parents were *REAL*. They sincerely loved God, and wanted to serve Him. They wanted to do whatever He wanted them to do."

Another day, I spoke with Steve, a young suburban pastor who is very obviously much wiser than his years. He said, "My parents were as real in church as they were at home. I remember times when I was three or four, going back to the back bedroom, seeing and hearing my dad praying. Right then, I knew it was important enough to my dad to pray. Christianity was not just something he did on Sundays. It was his *life.*"

A busy assistant pastor in a large city church, Robbie said, "My folks were the same at church as they were at home. I think that was really important. Your kids will listen to what you say, but they watch what you do much more."

A few weeks later I listened as Joanne, a 23 year old graduate from home school, told me, "My parents were real. Christianity was their life, and more than anything else that stuck out to me."

Herein lies perhaps one of our greatest challenges of parenting: that of really, truly, honestly believing what we *say* we believe as parents. If we are to change the world, it must begin at home. If we are to bring up young people who are passionate about living daily in the glorious presence of the Almighty God, then we must ourselves experience that same burning passion. It is *realness,* it is *true transparency,* and it is life.

To boil down the statistics, when I asked, "Is there anything your parents did or did not do that pointed you in the direction of serving God," 21% answered that the *realness of their parents' faith* was integral to their own belief, 20% answered that their *parents' consistency* was the most important quality, while fourteen percent reported that their *parents' faithfulness* played a primary role in their own personal faith.

I submit that these three qualities are so closely related because they stem from the same basic root: having a genuine, deep-rooted faith that displays itself in the individual's daily life. That being the case, I have chosen to combine the three qualities into the same basic category: *realness.* In this light, the responses of my godly second-generation Christians show overwhelmingly that 76% of the young people were impacted the most by their parents' REALNESS. This deeply ingrained quality exhibits itself in a working faith, a living love, and an abiding peace, and it changed forever the lives of those closest to them—their children.

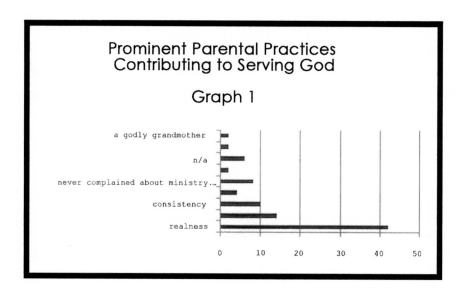

Prominent Parental Practices
Contributing to Serving God

Graph 1

So what exactly is *realness?*

It is not perfection; it is imperfection transparent. It is not having a perfect, problem-free life; it is having problems and really, truly, casting them upon the Lord. It is not working ourselves half to death in an attempt to prove our perfection; it is acknowledging our weaknesses and allowing Him to work through us.

The ancient tradition of the Olympic Flame became the longest and most popular relay in the world in the early 1900's. Lit from a concave mirror in Olympia, Greece, the flame is carried to the host city and is used to light the Olympic Caldron. The final torchbearer, who often symbolizes Olympic ideals, is kept a secret until the very last minute. By the time the flame reaches the stadium, excitement and fervor has reached a fever pitch. But in the 1956 Summer Olympics in Melbourne, Australia, something very surprising occurred.

On its way from Cairnes to Melbourne, the torch had already gone through several mishaps. Runners battled heat exhaustion, thunderous downpours, and a finicky flame. But it was in Sydney that the flame made Olympic history.

Harry Dillon, a cross-country titleholder, was supposed to take the flame to the mayor, Pat Hills, who was prepared to make a speech before passing the torch along to its next runner. Excitement ran high in Sydney, with 30,000 people lining the streets waiting for the torch to arrive.   Police escorts, reporters, and multitudes of anxious onlookers fidgeted in the tense moments.

Finally the runner emerged, carrying his flame with a proud, light step. Applause and cheers rippled through the crowd as they surged forward with cameras blazing to catch this momentous event. In an effort to protect the runner, the police surrounded him and escorted him as he lightly ran through the streets.

With the confidence of an athlete, the runner bounded up the steps and handed the flame to the waiting mayor. Mr. Hills smiled, thanked the runner, and turned toward the crowd, clearing his throat to make his speech. Before he could open his mouth, however, someone stepped up to him and whispered something startling:

"That's not the torch!"

The mayor looked startled and stared at the object in his hand. Suddenly it dawned on him that what he was holding was nothing but a chair leg topped with a plum-pudding can, with the "mighty Olympic flame" coming from a pair of kerosene-soaked underwear! The dignitaries on the platform looked around to find the mystery runner, but he had already disappeared into the throng.

What everyone thought was the real thing, was *not* the real thing. As a matter of fact, the prankster was so convincing that the police, the crowd, and even the mayor were all fooled!

Our Christian life can be a lot like that false Olympic torch. We can have lots of people convinced that we are really Christians, at least for a time. We can look like a Christian, act like a Christian, and even smell like a Christian . . . for awhile. We may have cameras clicking, the applause of the crowd, and a police escort, but someday *someone* will realize we don't have the real flame. Time reveals the truth.

As a matter of fact, our children are the first ones to notice whether we are truly *real* or not!
Steve put it this way: "Kids are smart—you can't pull anything over on them. They're just as human as we are. Young people know a real thing, instead of an imitation."

Awhile back, my family and I were at a church service in a heartland state when an elderly gentleman, Dr. Wells, stood up to speak. The crowd hushed as he stood shakily to his feet and spoke reverently about what the Lord had done in his life. Waving a trembling hand, he said softly, "My marriage was on the rocks. My wife and I were headed for a divorce, and my little boy was afraid of me because I didn't treat him very well. One day I got saved. I read the Bible for an hour that day, and I turned to the Bible for answers when people began asking me questions. Sometimes I would read for even eight hours a day—so much that my wife began to worry about me!"

He lowered his voice and continued, "One day after I had been saved for just a few weeks, I was sitting reading my Bible, and I saw out of the corner of my eye that my boy was on the couch on the other side of the room. He was still scared of me, you see. As I kept reading, I noticed that he edged his way closer and closer, till finally he was right beside me. 'Daddy,' he said, 'You're a new Daddy now, aren't you?' I looked at him, and tears filled my eyes as I told him, 'Yes, son. Jesus made me a new Daddy. I'm sorry I was such a wicked Daddy before, but Jesus changed my life, and now I'm a new Daddy. By God's Grace, that old Daddy will never come back.'"

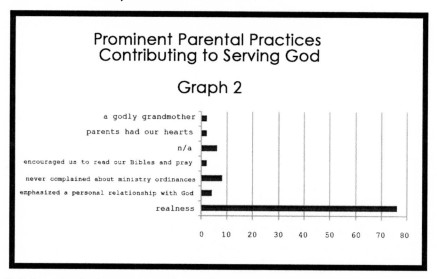

"My boy climbed up into my lap and pointed to the Bible. 'I love this Book, Daddy, because this Book tells about Jesus, and He's given me a new Daddy. Promise me you'll always read this Book and do what it says, because I don't want that old Daddy to come back.' Then he leaned over and kissed my Bible.

I promised him that I would always read this Book and do what it says. That old Daddy has never been back."

Brushing the tears from his eyes, the old man paused before continuing. "My boy called me the other day. He's married now, and has a family of his own. He said, 'Dad, I just wanted you to know that I love you, and I'm proud of you. You may not be able to do all the things you've wanted to do, but you've done everything you needed to. Thank you so much for being my dad and for being a wonderful example of a Christian for me.' Of course, I cried when he told me that. This next week, we'll be going to be with him, and we'll go to his church and worship God together. I thank God for what He's done in my life."

Dr. Wells had something *real* in his life, something life-changing that affected everything about him. It revolutionized his life, his marriage, and his parenting. It was completely transforming, because it was *real*!

All people need to see a real God at work, before they will put their trust in Him. Who better to show forth the marvelous handiwork of God than we Christians?

> "But ye are a chosen generation, a royal priesthood, an holy nation,
> a peculiar people; that ye should shew forth the praises of Him
> who hath called you out of darkness into His marvelous light." (1
> Pet. 2:9)

Each of us is the showroom of God's work, a display to others of what He can do in the life of a person.

Faith is a lot like learning to play an instrument. When I was young, I wanted to learn to play the guitar, so I began saving my money. I saved $5 a week—my entire allowance—for six whole months. I didn't even buy a candy bar! Finally, I had over $100 saved, and my dad took me to a pawn shop where I saw the most beautiful red Kay hummingbird six string guitar. It was big for me, but I told Dad that I wanted to grow into it. My, was I happy when I came home with that instrument! I simply loved that thing. I spent hours plucking the strings, making strange noises with it, and really getting nowhere. Finally, my mother found someone who could give me lessons, and I began to learn how to play my wonderful instrument. I remember how thrilled I was just to watch my instructor play. He showed me several different chords, and a few different ways of strumming. Watching him made me want to play even more. I thought to myself, *If he can do it, maybe I can do it too!*

After the first lesson, I was sent home to practice. It was strange, trying to play that thing myself, but it wasn't until I began to try <u>myself</u> that I really learned how to play. Then, it was only a matter of time before it became second nature to me. I didn't just know the instrument, I *knew* the instrument.

That's the way it is with faith: someone can explain it to you, and it's very hard to comprehend. But to watch someone else exercise faith and to see the Lord do something special for them gives you the courage to think, *If God can do that for them, maybe He'll do the same thing for me!* Finally comes the day when you exercise faith in the Lord, asking Him to help in a situation or work a miracle on your behalf, understanding that He is the only One who can do it. It is then that He steps from the ramparts of Heaven and meddles in the affairs of men long enough to bless you and give you the help that you need! Then you have really learned what faith is, and soon becomes second nature to you. You don't just trust God, you *trust* God.

It's the same way with our children. They are watching us daily to see how we respond to life's trials. How we as parents respond, and how God works in our lives, is something the children need to see.

First, our children need to see that **God's Presence** is a reality to us. As we live our daily lives knowing we are standing in the presence of a holy God, it will affect what we do, and ultimately what we allow the children to do.

One day I met with a very talented mother of two high-school boys. Normally a very quiet lady, Abby talked freely. "My parents knew that God was watching, and they wanted us to understand that as well. They were *very* consistent with us. It seems to me that their consistency helped me to see that God would not let me get away with stuff."

This was also illustrated in my meeting with an intelligent brunette schoolteacher named Angela. While she watched her class on the playground, we talked about her childhood as the youngest of three lively sisters, who amazingly are all in full-time Christian ministry. With her clear blue eyes twinkling, she said, "My sisters and I would sit around and actually discuss doing things we knew we shouldn't do. It's kinda funny looking back on it now. But every time, when the question came up, 'should we do this?' the answer we always came up with was, 'Nah—Mom would find out.' And I think that is one of the main reasons we are all serving God today: we knew we could not get away with stuff at home, and we knew that God wouldn't let us get away with stuff either. In our little minds, the 'fear of Mom' easily transferred to 'the fear of God.'"

Second, our children need to see that **God's Provision** is a reality to us. Several of my respondents told me how their parents' trust in God and His provision for their needs made a huge difference in their own faith.

Steve was quite frank about his childhood. His parents lived by faith, trusting God for their daily needs. Though every need was supplied, there had been some times when it looked bleak. But God always met the need…sometimes in very curious ways. After one particularly intense struggle with doubt, Steve was amazed to see God provide in a marvelous way. It changed his life. He told me, "Because I saw God provide for my parents like that, I had no doubt that He could provide for me, too!"

One of the ladies I spoke to, Tracy, spoke very tenderly of her parents, who are now elderly. A lovely young lady with a very large family, she seemed as happy as ever, with a deep trust in God that is rare to find. During our conversation, she alluded to the solid confidence her parents had in God's provision, and how it impacted her life. "My folks had a deep trust in God—almost unbelievable. Words could not express how much faith they had. Dad had vehicles given to him as a result of prayer. There were times when there was no food in the cupboard and Dad would say, 'The Lord will supply.' Sure enough, then someone would leave groceries on the front doorstep. There were times when we had our last five dollars, he would put it in the offering, and it was amazing! Someone would come after church and give him several hundred dollars! I knew it was because he gave to the Lord, and the Lord blessed him. To me, his trust in God connected that abstract thing called faith to my real life. It became a kind of security blanket to me; I began to trust in God through trust in my parents."

Thirdly, our children need to see that **God's Protection** is a reality to us. Do we trust in Him to protect us—and when He does, do we thank Him for the protection He has provided? When God's marvelous Hand shields us, our children need to see that we are quick to give Him the glory.

After church one day, I talked with a vivacious young evangelist's daughter, Suzanna. I had known her for years, and she was always excited about one thing or another. That day was no exception. "God has been so good to us!" she bubbled. "You would not believe what happened!" When I expressed my curiosity, she told me an incredible story of how God miraculously protected their motor home from catching fire recently, as well other occasions. Her conclusion was so startling, I ran for my computer to write it down as soon as I left the conversation. She said, "Maybe it was my parents' prayers, or maybe it was just God being merciful to us, but I've seen God work miracles, and I know I can trust Him." It is readily apparent that she saw God's handiwork, and it affected her deeply.

Another day, my family and I were at a church which was pastored by a young man named Nathan. We had been there before several times, and Nathan is a quiet kind of steady fellow that loves his family and his God. In the brief few minutes after the service that I talked with him, he shared some astonishing stories of how he saw God's Hand of protection.

"I saw God work in our family's life time after time, in incredible ways, in direct answer to prayer. There was no other way these things would have happened.

"One night when our whole family was in the van, Dad slowed down to take a right turn. The vehicle behind us pulled around, but the eighteen wheeler behind him didn't see us, so he plowed into us while he was still going about fifty-five miles an hour. I don't remember much about the crash, but I remember hearing my mother cry out, 'God, help us!' The van spun and rolled, and ended up in a field. The truck hit us so hard that our windshield blew out across the road from the impact. The back of the van cracked in half, and a part of the roof came down and hit me in the head.

"After everything came to a stop, the semi-truck driver grabbed a flashlight, got out of his truck and looked at the damage on the front of his truck, but went back into the truck, assuming we were all dead. He was really shook up; I guess he didn't want to see the bodies.

"Amazingly, we all walked away from that destroyed van, with only minor injuries. We all had some bumps, scrapes and bruises, but we also came away with an incredible awe of the mighty power of God. No one could have lived through that crash . . . but God protected us. It was a direct answer to Mom's prayer.

"Another time we were moving, and for some reason the brakes went out on the moving van. Dad was able to stop it at the top of a hill, but the transmission wasn't working right either, so it didn't go into park. We were all standing around outside while the tow truck was trying to hook it up. Suddenly, the big moving van began to roll backwards. It began gaining speed as it went down the hill. I couldn't believe it, but my ten-year old brother got behind it, thinking he could stop it. Before we knew it, somehow, something knocked him out of the way. We saw him fly sideways through the air and roll through the grass, completely unharmed. To this day, we think it had to have been an angel, pushing him out of the way. We were so relieved when the truck ran into a hill, bringing it to a stop.

"We assumed most everything inside the van was busted up, but eventually, we found out that almost all our glass items were still intact! One of the only things that broke was a picture with the words, 'Except ye repent, ye shall all likewise perish.' My parents never fixed it, they just hung it up, broken, to remind us all of God's goodness."

Nathan looked at me and said, "I saw God was real in my parents' lives, and it affects me to this day!"

Finally, our children need to see that **God's Power** for living a godly life is real to us. When we go through trials and hardships, is God's power real? Do we trust Him to help us through?

Maureen, a self-proclaimed "daddy's girl," said that it was her father who first showed her the power of God.

"My dad has always had physical problems," she explained. "He was given some experimental medications as he was growing up, and it caused the bones in his legs to begin deteriorating as he got older. He also began developing other issues, and it seemed like he was always in pain. Often, he had trouble getting around. Still, he kept on going. Because he was field representative for a prison ministry, he did a lot of traveling. Many times he battled with physical problems, and sometimes it seemed like he couldn't go on—but he did. He just kept on going, even through the pain and suffering.

"God gave my dad the power and strength to do what He wanted him to do. To me, it only seems reasonable that I can trust God and rely on His power as well. If God could help my dad, He can do it for me too."

Maureen learned to see God's fingerprints in her parents' lives.

Like Maureen, our young people are watching us. They long to see real life examples of someone living out the principles of the Bible. Seeing God work marvelously is essential to building faith. But the miracle must happen in us, the parents. When a young person sees God's handiwork in another's life, they think, *Could God do the same for me?* The Bible comes alive! It is no longer just a storybook; it is a Book to be read, learned, and trusted in everyday life! It is loved because it is the Word of GOD, who is that miracle-worker in their life.

Young people need to see God at work—somewhere!

The sorcerers of Egypt cared little about Moses and his God until Moses showed them a miracle they could not imitate. *THEN,* they exclaimed, "This is the finger of God!" (Ex. 8:19) People will only see a real God when He has done something for someone that they know the person could not do for themselves. Seeing a changed life, answered prayer, and other blessings which can only be attributed to a real God all help produce that faith-bringing "light bulb moment". When we go through a trial and God works a miracle, whether He gives us the grace to deal with the issue or whether He delivers us from it, it is shown before others as The Hand of God.

The finger of God is something that cannot be duplicated. It is like the Olympic Flame: real, constant, and moving. It is a living, breathing reality which is difficult to explain, let alone understand, but it is nonetheless real. It is the difference between merely looking at a photo of the ocean, and actually smelling the salty air, listening to the pounding waves, and feeling the cool spray. It is the difference between hearing about the joys of parenthood, and actually feeling the weight of your newborn as the nurse lays her in your arms, all squalling, gooey, and . . . beautiful! It is the difference between merely seeing, and BEING. It is life itself!

Therefore, could it be that God allows difficult situations in our lives as parents, so that we can reach out by faith and let God do miracles—thereby being the examples that our children so desperately need? Absolutely!

> ". . . things which happened unto me have fallen out rather unto the furtherance of the gospel . . . " (Philippians 1:12).

> "Who comforteth us in all our tribulation, that we may be able to comfort them which are in any trouble, by the comfort wherewith we ourselves are comforted of God"(2 Corinthians 1:4).

This quality of *realness* is so important that it was mentioned by 76% of my respondents. That means that these godly young people felt that their parents' transparency was one of the most, if not THE most, important quality that pointed them toward serving the Lord.

> Mom taught us to be real. This is perhaps the main reason why each of us attends church or is in the ministry today. The Mom we watched at church as the pastor's wife was the same person we saw at home. Christianity was not a game we played on Sundays and Wednesdays. It was who we were. We did what we did, not because people were watching us, but because what we did was the right thing to do.
>
> Mom taught us these lessons and many others, not by telling them to us, but by living them in front of us each and every day of her life; and they are lessons that I will never forget.[5]

So here is some good news for those of you who wonder whether you have what it takes to raise a godly young person: *you do not have to be perfect, just real.*

Take the time to examine yourself—your life, your heart, your spirit – and ask God to show you the truth. Have you *truly* been born-again? Has there been a time in your life when you have humbled yourself before God and sought His forgiveness, thanking Him for His sacrificial death? There is no room for pretend Christians in this battle for the souls of our young people. (See Appendix A, The Real Thing for more information.)

As you sincerely love the Lord and desire to please Him . . . at home, at church, at school, at work, in the store, on the phone, on the computer, and in the virtual world, you will find the realness of His <u>presence</u>, His <u>provision</u>, His <u>protection</u>, and His <u>power </u>become apparent in *your* life.

It is the finger of God, which cannot be duplicated. It is your primary protection, without which there is no defense. It is *realness*, and it is life.

LIONPROOF STRATEGY #1:
BE REAL!

PREPARING YOUR DEFENSE

1.   What are your goals for your children? If you've never thought about it before, now is the time to think about it. Take your time as you complete this; pray about it and talk to your spouse. Then write out your goals for future reference.

2.   How has being born again impacted your life? Have there been differences in your desires since you've been saved? Write about what God did for you when you trusted Christ, and don't forget to take some time to thank Him for the marvelous work of grace He has done!

3.   Think about a time in your life when you saw someone go through a difficult situation and God worked wonderfully in their life. How did that affect you? Did your trust in God grow as a result of their example? Write about it.

4.   How do you think God could use your experiences in the lives of your children?

ASSIGNMENT:

Set aside some time to share your experiences with your family, and check the boxes when you have done it!

- [ ] Your born-again experience
- [ ] A time when God provided something or met a need in your life.
- [ ] A time you know God protected you from danger, or worked a miracle on your behalf.
- [ ] A time when God helped you through a problem or a trial.

Memory Verse:

"We will not hide them from their children, shewing to the generation to come the praises of the LORD, and his strength, and his wonderful works that he hath done."(Psalm 78:4)

THOUGHT QUESTIONS for chapter 4:

1. What do you think made Christianity attractive to you?

2. What, in your opinion, makes Christianity appealing to others?

3. What impact does one individual's sourness, grouchiness, and selfishness have on others?

CHAPTER 4:
STRENGTHENING YOUR DEFENSE

It's not that the outside influences are too strong, it's that the inside fortifications are too weak.—David Cloud

" . . . for the joy of the LORD is your strength."(Nehemiah 8:10c)

"But godliness with contentment is great gain." (1 Timothy 6:6)

Joy is a powerful influence for good, and a deterrent to evil. Being one of the very first fruits of the Spirit, true inner joy is a quality that Satan despises. It is so powerful, in fact, that the Lord says that it is your strength!

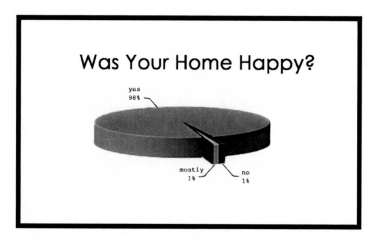

In raising godly Christian young people, joy in parenting is a must! It is like raising a tall, stout wall of defense in the lives of our children. Many of the second-generation Christians I interviewed told of their parents' joy, and the impact it had on their lives.

While in the northwest one spring, I met Shari, a young assistant pastor's wife with two small rambunctious children. Her late father was the pastor of a mid-sized country church, where her parents had ministered for 20 years. Shari, a fourth generation Christian, is part of a remarkable family with all six adult children serving the Lord. Her parents' attitude was that serving the Lord was the best thing in the world.

"My parents simply loved serving the Lord," she told me. "They truly enjoyed everything they did for God, whether it was soul-winning, bus visitation, cleaning the church, counseling, or anything. It wasn't just 'working in the church.' To them, it was serving the Lord, and it was the most wonderful thing in the world. I guess I grew up thinking the same thing. It seemed to me to be the best thing ever; it was all I wanted to do with my life."

Shari's sentiments were not at all unusual. A vast majority of the godly people I talked to felt exactly the same way. In fact, 98% of my respondents said their home was happy!

Let me remind you that these young people know why they are now serving the Lord. It is not rocket science, nor is it merely a theory; it is the principles of Scripture lived out in the lives of their parents that made all the difference. In some cases, like Shari's, we see generation after generation of joyful Christians that have impacted the world.

First, let's look at the negative. It's a well-known fact that parental stress has a harmful effect on children. A 2003 article from the University of Washington states:

> Elementary school children whose parents experienced symptoms of poor mental health or high parental aggravation (parents who feel stressed or angry toward their children) were almost five times as likely to have severe emotional and behavioral problems as children whose parents reported better mental health or only moderate aggravation. For adolescents, the risk of having severe emotional and behavioral problems was almost three times greater if a parent experienced symptoms of poor mental health or high

levels of aggravation. Similarly, parents were about five times more likely to report mental health challenges if they had a child with severe emotional and behavioral problems.

As they looked for possible causes of parental stress and anger, researchers found that many factors contribute to poor parental mental health, including economic hardship, single parenting, unemployment, not completing high school, having a teenager in the house, and latchkey child care. [6]

With his .303 and slug-loaded shotgun both securely in position, Lieutenant Colonel John Patterson waited in the intense darkness. The late jemedar's tent was close by, and the colonel was hoping the lion would come back to the same spot for another meal. He strained his ears for any sound of just one of the huge beasts.

It wasn't long before his wait was rewarded . . . a menacing roar came closer and closer. Soon, however, there was silence—an ominous, inky-dark silence. Patterson shifted his weight uneasily in his tree stand, scalp prickling and eyes straining in the darkness.

Silence. It always precedes the attack.

A study conducted by Dr. Wyman, associate professor at the University of Rochester, states that:

> [...] research has shown links between chronic parent stress and children's emotional well-being. [7]

Another article from the University of Rochester Medical Center puts it this way:

> Children whose parents and families are under ongoing stress have
> more fevers with illness than other children. [8]

So, if a child's physical and mental health is affected by the parents' attitude, should it come as a surprise that spiritual health also depends greatly on parents? The atmosphere we create in our homes can be a toxic one, or it can be a healthy one. It all depends on us. It may be helpful to us to realize:

> Complaints are poison.

> Unthankfulness is cancerous.

> Criticism is corrosive.

"Did your Dad complain?" I asked Robbie. "Never," he replied emphatically. "How about your Mom?" I wondered. He thought for a minute and then answered, "No, not that I can remember." Amazingly, 56% of my respondents reported that their parents NEVER complained, and 24% claimed that their parents RARELY complained. Lest you think those I interviewed are perfect, a few said that one of their parents sometimes complained, and a small fraction reported that their parents regularly complained. However, when you look at the numbers, it's a whopping 80% of non- or rarely complaining parents!

Does this mean that these folks never had anything to complain about? Hardly.

"My parents had a lot of hardships, raising us seven kids," Lance told me. The son of a pastor, he is one of the older children of a large family. His mother had recently succumbed to cancer, after a short but brutal battle, leaving his father with several children still at home.

"With a passel of very active boys and one special-needs child, there was always something going on. We kids knew they must have had financial troubles, but we never heard about them."

Lance ran his fingers through his hair and continued thoughtfully. "As far as gossip, we probably had that, too, but somehow it didn't affect us kids. Our church had a big split one time while we were young, but we were careful not to listen to the gossip."

Through hardship, pain, gossip, financial strain, and even death many families just like Lance's refused to complain. In return, they have a happy, well-adjusted family. I think that's a wise investment.

So I asked him a more probing question. "Would you say your parents were content? Were they generally satisfied with their life?" He answered with a smile, "Yes, I really think they were. Of course, they always wanted to improve themselves, but they were satisfied with their lives." Not surprisingly, Lance's answer was very consistent with the rest of the interviewees: 78% said that their parents were content.

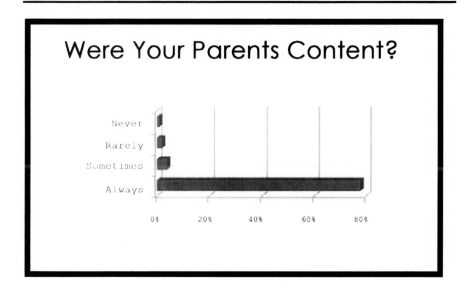

How could Lance's parents be content, even in the hard times? I don't think it comes naturally. The truth of Scripture speaks on this issue:

> **"In every thing** give thanks: for this is the will of God in Christ Jesus concerning you" (1 Thessalonians 5:18).

> "Rejoice in the Lord **always**: and again I say, Rejoice" (Philippians 4:4).

> "Be careful for nothing; but in every thing by prayer and supplication **with thanksgiving** let your requests be made known unto God" (Philippians 4:6).

> Casting **all** your care upon him; for he careth for you. (1 Peter 5:7)

"My mom was a wonderful example to us," Lance told me. "When she was diagnosed with cancer, she began to count every day as a bonus. Even when she lost her hair, she never complained. And when she died a short six months later, my dad grieved, but never once did he accuse God of making a bad move. He felt that God knew what He was doing. Her example and his testimony are very powerful, even today."

If you are a habitual complainer, ask God to help you stop, before you open the door for Satan to come into your house and drag away your little ones. Never forget that God knows exactly what He is doing. Start each day with a smile, and end it with praise, even if it is through tears. Eventually, you will have formed the habit of joyfulness, and your life will happier by the day. Before you know it, your family will be smiling with you, and your defense against the wicked one will be stronger than ever.

LIONPROOF STRATEGY #2:
BE JOYFUL!

STRATEGY #3:
BE CONTENT!

PREPARING YOUR DEFENSE:

1. What is real joy? Real joy is not ecstasy, mere "feeling good", an adrenaline rush, warm fuzzies or nostalgia, or just having a good day. It is not a happiness that depends on the outward circumstances; rather, it is a an abiding fullness in the soul associated with:

   o A sense of <u>security</u> surrounding what is most important to you

   o A sense of <u>affection</u>: being loved, with opportunities to love back

   o A sense of great <u>expectations</u> for the future—I WILL BE TAKEN CARE OF, I WILL BE HAPPY!

   o A sense that <u>life counts</u>—I have been given a job that is worthwhile

2. Where is real joy to be found?

   o In salvation! Without the Lord, there can be no joy! (See John 15:11; 2 Corinthians 3:17) If there is no joy in your life, there may not be a real salvation.

   o In God's Presence! *"Thou wilt shew me the path of life: in thy presence is fulness of joy; at thy right hand there are pleasures for evermore." (Psalm 16:11).* It's very easy to work for God without being in God's presence. If you know for certain that you're a born-again Christian (see Appendix A: The Real Thing) and you still have no joy, carefully evaluate your priorities, and see if there is anything out of line with God's priorities.

3. What are barriers to joy?

   o Sourness and self-will—expressions of perfectionistic expectations that cannot be fulfilled in an imperfect world!

   o Sin! David describes the misery of having sin in his life in Psalm 51. When there is sin in your life, God will not listen to your prayers. And if God doesn't hear you, it's a miserable existence!

4. What are boosts to joy?

   o Who is an earthly helper? See 2 Corinthians 1:24.

o What is a Heavenly helper (in addition to the Holy Spirit)? See Jeremiah 15:16.

5. Deuteronomy chapter 28 outlines the blessings that accompany obedience to the Lord, and the curses that come upon God's people when they do not obey Him. Verse 47 is a key verse in this chapter, and perfectly addresses the average Christian in the western culture. We have been abundantly blessed—above any people group that has ever lived on this planet—and we should be able to serve the Lord with joy!

THOUGHT QUESTIONS FOR CHAPTER 5:

1. Do you believe in the permanency of marriage?

2. How important is faithfulness to you?

3. Do you think that how young people perceive a marriage is important?

CHAPTER 5:
"STRENGTH THROUGH UNITY"
(Motto, Houston Corps of Cadets, ROTC)[9]

"Lord, we are not interested in being famous or wealthy, but what
we would like is to dedicate our children that come from this
union to You. We will serve You all the days of our lives, and all the
pay that we would want is to have our children serve You, too."[10]

*"Two are better than one; because they have a good reward for their labour. For if they
fall, the one will lift up his fellow: but woe to him that is alone when he falleth; for he
hath not another to help him up. Again, if two lie together, then they have heat: but how
can one be warm alone? And if one prevail against him, two shall withstand him; and a
threefold cord is not quickly broken." (Ecclesiastes 4:9-12)*

At a friend's funeral, I was thrilled to see her remarkable legacy of nine
children and thirty-eight grandchildren, many of whom are being raised in
the ministry. Each of her children and most of her grandchildren have put
their faith and trust in the Lord Jesus Christ and are living their lives for Him.
Mary has been a wonderful testimony of a godly wife and mother.

I would have never guessed, however, that her marriage hadn't always been
wonderful. In their early marriage, the fights were almost constant and Mary
wondered if she had made a terrible mistake. Still, Mary and her husband were
unwilling to get a divorce, so they turned to God and began attending church.

God graciously rewarded their search for truth by leading them both to trust Him for salvation. Now that they were born-again, they began to seek Him for every decision. Through His Word, they discovered that as they drew closer to God, they drew closer to each other. It created a strong foundation for stable, happy children.

A Child's Perception

In my talks with second generation Christians, I discovered that the very vast majority of them (89%) perceived their parents' marriage as excellent. Some, five percent, rated their parents' marriage as good, while just as many stated their parents' marriage was average. The conclusion is not surprising: when a child perceives stability in the marriage, it creates steadiness in his life.

That is not to say that disagreements or fights never happen; in fact, arguing is an inevitable part of married life. My respondents had several classifications for their parents:

- Those that had terrible marriages before they got saved
- Those that occasionally fight
- Those that never have a conflict in front of the children, but have their "discussions" behind closed doors
- However, by far, the most common response of the young person was, "I never knew there were any problems!"

Could it really be true that these young people had no idea there were any problems or difficulties in their parents' lives? After all, I knew most of these parents personally for many years; I knew that they experienced many trials which affected their marriages: challenges of a financial nature, or physical problems, or people talking about them. However, the perception of the young people is that, "I had no idea there were any problems" (see Chapter 4: Strengthening Your Defense.) I submit that the style of arguing is more important than whether or not the arguing took place.

A 2007 New York Times article reports that:

> "Recent studies show that how often couples fight or what they fight about usually doesn't matter. Instead, it's the nuanced interactions between men and women, and how they react to and

resolve conflict, that appear to make a meaningful difference in the
health of the marriage and the health of the couple."[11]

Micah, an athletic young youth pastor, took a break from his busy schedule to explain, "In our home, there was usually a positive attitude, not an atmosphere of depression. We never felt like there was a cloud over us." Micah's parents learned to address their concerns without hostility and without doing emotional damage. In so doing, they did not ruin the mood of the whole house with their differing opinions.

While many of my respondents reported that they could not recall their parents arguing, some had a different story. One very observant young lady, Abigail, said, "My parents have a good marriage, I would say. Not excellent, but it is good. Sometimes my parents would fight as we were growing up. Not real, physical fights, but they got into some pretty heated arguments. Their marriage is good overall, but it has its rough spots."

Tracy told me, "I would say my parents had a good marriage; it wasn't really excellent, but it wasn't bad either. My mother likes to run things, and that's not very good. Unfortunately, my parents didn't keep the fighting in the bedroom, but they always came to some sort of agreement. Both my parents had a tremendous desire to do whatever the Lord wanted, and often that seemed to settle the disputes."

How was your parents' marriage?

- excellent - 89%
- good - 5%
- average - 5%
- poor - 1%

89%   5%   1% 5%

So if you argue occasionally and even in front of the children, know that you are in good company. Not that these testimonies justify arguing, but they show us that successful godly parents have the same trials and temptations that befall all of us . . . but they learned to address their concerns without doing harm, availing themselves of the strength and power of God to embrace their God-given roles, and occasionally to agree to disagree.

Parents' Wisdom

There are a few more important items of note concerning the marriages of successful parents. One is that, in a successful-parent marriage, the spouses back up each other's decisions. They present a unified position to the children. When one parent makes a rule, the other parent agrees to it and enforces it, just as the other would do. They support each other in every aspect of their home.

Brittany is from an amazing family. Being fifth generation Christians, she and her brothers are all involved in ministry – she is a youth pastor's wife, and both her brothers are music ministers in their respective churches. With her two children clamoring about her, she voiced her experience in this area. "My mom stood behind Dad in everything," she said gravely. "They were unified in their rules and in their enforcement."

In The Complete Idiot's Guide to a Well-Behaved Child, Ericka Lutz writes, "In 'public,' in front of your kids, consistency is vital. If you're not consistent, your kids are going to play you off, one parent against another. You need to develop a unified front, that is, an agreed approach to the issues." We may not always agree on an approach, a limit, or a consequence, but we can plan ahead for the times when we disagree.

Another important point uncovered in my interviews is that the parents said positive things about each other. They never tore each other down in public, and especially not in front of the children. They knew that to tear down their spouse is to tear down themselves.

Joanne told me about a dear friend of hers who is away from God now. "I had a friend that I was really close to," she said quietly. "Unfortunately, his mom never backed up his dad. She was always supplanting him, belittling him, and running him down, even in front of the children. Even I noticed it, though I was just a friend. It really affected my friend; I can see to this day that God's not real to him. It was really bad for him."

Let us learn from people like Mary and her husband. They didn't always have an ideal marriage, but they sought the Lord and did their best to obey Him in their roles as husband and wife. They learned to communicate with each other without animosity, to present a unified front, and to speak positively about their spouse. They learned what the Bible says and began doing it. And because they did, there are now many young people across the globe living as a light for those around them. Oh, to have a legacy like theirs!

LIONPROOF STRATEGY #4:
BE UNIFIED!

PREPARING YOUR DEFENSE:

1. Take some time to reflect on your wedding vows. What were they? Did you pledge "'till death do us part?" Read Malachi 3, and think about the phrase, *"that He might seek a godly seed."* What do you think that means?

2. Based on this chapter, what are some further steps you can take to reinforce your marriage? Can you learn better how to handle disagreements?

3. How do you think your children perceive your marriage? If your answer is "I have no idea!" or, "well, probably average," are you willing to do what's necessary to improve it?

Specific Assignments:

1. Most couples argue about three basic things: child training, finances, or the physical relationship. Knowing this, read a good Christian book on one of these topics, preferably with your spouse. If it has a workbook or exercises, try to make sure you do these.

   ☐ check when completed

2. Try to do something, no matter how small, for your spouse every day. Perhaps it is something as simple as making him a cup of coffee, or as elaborate as a special night together. Whatever you do, try to take a bit of time to express your love.

Patterson and his men were back on the hunt for the lion, taking up positions in trees at night and rummaging through the jungles in the daytime. His nerves were frayed, however, and the colonel could not much longer endure such a strain as this. Heartbroken, dejected, and utterly weary, he felt like giving up.

But he couldn't. Too many lives were depending on him. "As long as there is a lion out there and I have breath in my body, I will NEVER give up. I WILL go on. I WILL get those lions, if it is the last thing I do!"

The light of dawn was filtering through the trees when a man broke through the clearing. "Simba! Simba!" he screamed.

"Where?" Patterson's eyes narrowed.

"Down by the river," the man shrieked, waving his arms. "He tried to get one of the men there, but he got a donkey instead. He's down there right now, eating it!"

By the time the man finished his frenzied plea, Patterson had gathered his firearms and was running out the door. "Come show me where he is!" he called back over his shoulder. The frightened man followed as quickly as he could.

Quietly they approached the place where they could hear the crunching of bones and a faint purring. Soon, the colonel could make out the outline of the animal through the thick brush. He was about to lower his rifle into position when his friend stepped on a rotten twig, snapping it noisily. The lion looked up, growled in warning, and escaped into the forest . . . again.

"I am NOT letting him go this time!" Patterson told his guide. "I will get him . . . today!" Running his fingers through his hair, he said, "He'll probably come back to finish his meal. I'm setting up right here!" He secured the remains of the donkey, then, since there were no trees close by, he built a twelve foot platform just a few yards away from the body. With that, he settled in, for darkness was coming. Soon the beast would return.

This time, Patterson was alone. It was so dark. And quiet. He grew weary. Until he heard a noise that made his scalp prickle. A twig snapped, and he heard a large body pushing its way through the bushes. But then, the lion stopped and gave a low, menacing growl. He knew Patterson was there, and he didn't like it.

Patterson feared that the lion would turn and run, like usual. But instead, the lion ignored the donkey and began stalking him! The next two hours were agony, as the lion stealthily circled the platform, creeping closer, ever closer. Patterson knew the platform was flimsy, and that the lion could easily spring the twelve feet that separated him from his prey. The very thought made the man's skin tingle.

His nerves jangling and eyes burning, Patterson was hardly prepared for what happened next. Smack! An object struck him in the back of the head! He convulsed with terror, thinking the lion had sprung on him from behind. But then he realized that it was nothing more than an owl, who thought he was a branch. The lion growled ominously.

It was with great difficulty that Patterson kept himself still after this. He trembled almost uncontrollably, as the beast continued to stalk him. But with eyes straining into the dark, the colonel soon realized he could make out the monster's outline in the jungle growth. Before death could approach any nearer, Patterson steadied himself, carefully sighted in his rifle and pulled the trigger.

The monster let out a tremendous roar as the bullet found its mark. Though the lion whirled turned and tried to run away, Patterson kept firing bullets into the overgrowth. The lion began loudly moaning, and then there were a few deep sighs. Finally, all was still.

The first of the great man-eating beasts was dead.

There was one more left.

PART THREE

YOUR OFFENSIVE WEAPONS

What you DO

THOUGHT QUESTIONS FOR CHAPTER 6:

1. Think back to when you were growing up. What or who do you think was the most formative influence in your childhood?

2. What or who do you think is the most formative influence in your children's lives?

3. In your opinion, how does a child's environment affect him?

CHAPTER 6:
BUILDING A BARRICADE

Better guide well the young than reclaim them when old,
For the voice of true wisdom is calling.
"To rescue the fallen is good, but 'tis best
To prevent other people from falling."
Better close up the source of temptation and crime
Than deliver from dungeon or galley;
Better put a strong fence 'round the top of the cliff
Than an ambulance down in the valley.
—taken from the poem, "A Fence or an Ambulance,"
by Joseph Malins (1895)[12]

If one bear holy flesh in the skirt of his garment, and with his skirt do touch bread, or pottage, or wine, or oil, or any meat, shall it be holy? And the priests answered and said, No. Then said Haggai, If one that is unclean by a dead body touch any of these, shall it be unclean? And the priests answered and said, It shall be unclean. (Haggai 2:12-13)

Jamie, a talkative middle-aged Sunday School teacher, had no trouble filling our 2 hour conversation with stories of her childhood. Her parents have served the Lord for well over 30 years, and there was a lot of adventure, fun, and love. Her stories were quite colorful.

Was hers a model family? Hardly. If you could go back in time, you would see a miserable man with a shrill wife. Her father, Rich, was a beer truck driver and was making good money, but he was wanted by the police and had a contract on his life. In fact, he had a few illegal activities on the side which netted him more money than his regular job.

"I remember sitting in a comfy chair and looking out the window," Jamie told me. "I was six years old at the time. My mom was real sad because Dad wasn't home. Then, when he came home, I was sent to bed real quickly. Looking back on it now, I know that Mom did that because Dad was drunk. I guess the main thing I remember about those days is how sad my mom was."

Rich and Jean had a nice house, a good income, and two sweet children. But he was an alcoholic, and his wife was just about at her wit's end. Then one day at a little church along a river, they met the Savior, and He changed their lives completely and forever.

"Although I was only little at the time, I remember how dramatically my parents' lives changed," Jamie went on to explain. "They went one hundred percent for the Lord, absolutely head first. Anything that they felt was good or godly they began incorporating into their lives, and everything that may have remotely been considered wrong they walked away from. They made some tremendous adjustments very quickly, and have never wavered since. Their consistency over the years has had an incredible impact on my life."

By God's grace, Rich and Jean built a barricade around their precious family, making them LIONPROOF and preventing their children from being taken without warning. They realized how easily Satan sneaks in to deceive people through the philosophies of the world. They created a barrier—boundaries that distinguished right from wrong—that protected their children from sin and defeat. Like Rich and Jean, parents of the second-generation Christians that I interviewed <u>all</u> shared something in common: they tried to prevent the Devil from destroying their children through his worldly influences.

My last two chapters have discussed what we need to BE in order to raise children who will follow God. Here is the chapter everyone's been waiting for: what to DO to raise godly children. But let me caution you not to sacrifice the internal on the altar of the external; the heart MUST be right before the externals have any meaning whatsoever. I almost hesitate to write this section, because I fear someone will think this is the most important thing. (In fact, there may be a few readers who literally skimmed the book, looking for just this information!) To those who are concerned primarily with externals over and above heart attitudes, I urge you to seriously consider the outcome of such a philosophy. Though some people I talked to experienced that form of parenting, their childhoods were not very happy. You can read their stories in the chapter titled "Exceptions."

An animated youth pastor, Brandon explained, "Rules—standards—existed, but they were not the central theme of my home. My parents didn't focus on rules; they focused on the Lord."

I also hesitate to write this section because there will be some reading this who may not be "doing all the right things," and will feel as though they could not possibly raise children to live for God. Let me emphasize that God can use an imperfect parent more than one who thinks they have it all together.

> He hath shewed thee, O man, what is good; and what doth the
> LORD require of thee, but to do justly, and to love mercy, and to
> walk humbly with thy God? (Micah 6:8)

Although some interviews left me feeling that I am the worst parent on earth, most did not. Interestingly, the people I talked to knew their parents well, and they understood that they were not perfect. These young people saw their parents in every situation, and are still living for God. It does not take a perfect parent to raise a godly child, only a parent who loves God and wants to serve Him.

With this in mind, we must recognize the importance of sheltering our children from harmful influences.

Were you sheltered as a child?
100% responded
YES

Arianna, a red-headed Christian school teacher, made this statement: "One of the things I feel very strongly about is protecting children. I simply don't think many people realize how vital it is to shelter young people from the manipulation of the Devil."

Arianna's answer was typical of these godly young people. ONE HUNDRED PERCENT of them were sheltered while they were growing up.

In what ways were they sheltered? Well, in many different ways, but they generally fall into four basic categories: spiritual foundation, entertainment, friendships, and music.

SPIRITUAL FOUNDATION

The foundation of the barricade: God's House

God's House was the foundation of these families. Involvement in church activities was assumed, and many of the children were actively involved in ministry themselves as they were growing up. Quite a few of them were involved as families in singing, working a bus route, going on visitation, etc.

Though one lion was gone, the other still prowled the camps. Some of the workers approached Patterson's tent. As the Lieutenant Colonel opened the flap, a large man stepped forward, glaring hard at his employer. "The men have all met together and decided that we cannot work here under these conditions," he announced. "We did not come here to become food for lions; we came here to work. If we cannot work in safety, we will not work at all."

Patterson glanced around from one man to another. He sighed, understanding their fear. But he had a job to do, and he must get it done. "I understand," he spoke quietly. "But before you give up completely, let's try to find ways to make your tents safer. Come in, and I will give you some ideas."

All regular work on the bridge ceased for several days while the men made extraordinarily thick and high bomas, or fences, around each camp. Then, as darkness descended, each stockade had a large fire, and the watchmen made a regular racket by clanging several tins together throughout the night. In this way, Patterson and the men hoped to frighten the lions.
Olympic Gold Medalist

You may be wondering, "How can this be part of Sheltering?" It's what is called Opportunity Cost. Look at it this way: if you have $20, and you go to the store and see a new jacket (price tag: $20), and a new shirt (you guessed it, price tag: $20!), you have a dilemma. For some of us, that's a serious problem! If you buy the one, you cannot buy the other. You have an opportunity, but it costs you another opportunity. It is an Opportunity Cost.

It's the same way with time. We all have twenty-four hours in a day to do what needs to be done. If we choose to spend our time doing one thing, we cannot do another. If we choose to spend our time at the House of God, we will usually not have time to be involved in other things such as organized sports, local civil activities, scouts, or other secular endeavors.

I'm not saying these things are necessarily wrong; I'm merely saying that our second-generation Christians who are serving God today are doing so because their time was invested in the service of the Lord. It became their way of life while they were young, and they continued on that path. The habits instilled by the parents are continued to this day.

Rachel, a third–generation Christian, is intensely passionate for God and her family. "I guess I would say, I always knew that while I was under my parent's roof, I would serve the Lord," she told me. "But when I got saved as a young girl, I wanted to serve the Lord myself.

"My dad told people that even if you would take away the fact that God exists, there would still be no better lifestyle than the Christian life. That always stuck with me. I knew that choosing the Christian life was choosing the *best* life."

Her husband, Jeff, also a third-generation Christian, added, "For me, it was a decision I made when I became a man. I realized that that was the life I wanted to live. Now we're living the Christian life together," he said as he slipped his arm around his wife.

Shari summarized the feelings of many when she said, "I simply never wanted to live any other kind of life. I saw the way my parents lived and how happy they were, and I knew that that's what I wanted for me."

As a constant drizzle soaks the land with life-giving water, so a steady flow of the Word of God softens little hearts. Though we realize that our children can slide right off a church pew into Hell, they must do so over the Word of God.

Also, because church was a priority, these people made the majority of their spiritual commitments either in church, or because of church.

With glowing eyes, Rachel expressed how the Lord worked in her heart. "I had been attending church all my life, being a pastor's kid. But when I was six or seven, I remember being in church, and the Lord said to me, 'Rachel, you're a good girl, but you're not saved.' I didn't get saved right then. I went home and talked to my dad, and told him that I felt convicted, but I didn't get saved then, either. In my child mind, I thought I had to go back to church. *Next Sunday,* I said to myself, *I'll get saved.* I don't remember the service, but I remember bowing my head and talking to God. I thought maybe I didn't understand, but the Lord said, 'You *are* older – a week older – and you need to be saved.' I remember saying out loud, 'All right, Lord.' I went out into the aisle to go forward, and it felt like I crawled to the altar. A deacon asked me if I wanted to be saved, and I told him, 'Yes.' I remember crying and praying, and then I remember the sin weight being *gone!* I knew just as sure as I'm sitting here that He forgave me of my sins, and I got saved. I was so happy and skipping inside!"

Jay is a talented singer, pianist, and assistant pastor at his suburban church. Never with a lack for friends, he and his wife are cheerful, happy people. During our interview one summer afternoon, Jay told me, "One thing my parents did was to take us all to church. We were always in church. It was very important to our family. We were in church and in Christian school, so I heard a lot of preaching growing up. As a very young boy I was lying in bed one night, and I was convicted that I was a sinner on my way to hell. I was by myself, and asked the Lord to save me." Jay paused for a moment, then said thoughtfully, "His working in my heart as a youngster completely set the direction for the rest of my life."

As a multitude of others would testify, Jay is where he is today because of the working of the Holy Spirit through the preaching of the Word he heard when he was very young.

In addition, church was a place of dedication, where many folks committed their life to serve the Lord. This was true in the life of Susan, a preacher's daughter who is now a missionary. She said, "The highlight of the year for our church was the annual Missions Conference. We went all out to get people excited and involved in missions, to get to know the missionaries, and to learn about their fields. But one year was different than the rest. It seemed as though the Lord was speaking right to *me* about the mission field! That week I went forward and prayed, dedicating my life to serve God. Now I'm a missionary myself, and I love it."

Even summer church camp can be a place of commitment. Jennifer is now a Christian school teacher and wife of the principal. Her teen years were somewhat turbulent, but eventually she found peace. "The Lord had been getting my attention through difficult times, but when I went to church camp, I seriously began to consider His purpose for my life. I had been starting in a bad direction, but the Lord changed me and directed me to live for Him."

For many of these people, church attendance became more than just "going to church;" it became the springboard for all their important life decisions—the foundation of their character. Their parents carefully built their barrier board by board, nail by nail, church service by church service, commitment by commitment.

Over time, their barrier helped to make them LIONPROOF.

Securing the barrier: Family Devotions

During one point in our ministry, our growing family was privileged to live in a small place in the country. It was the perfect place to have animals, and I bought some downy chicks. They were the cutest little things, and grew to be fat and fluffy hens, eventually laying the best speckled eggs! One day, however, I heard a lot of noise and commotion coming from the henhouse. When I got there, I was aghast to see a huge snake trying desperately to escape get out! Having swallowed two chickens, he was now too large to fit through his entryway. I ran to the kitchen, grabbed my butcher knife, and delivered a fatal jab behind his head.

Later, as I inspected the henhouse, I found about an inch and a half of slack in the chicken wire, enough to let a good sized snake through. Unfortunately for the two ingested chickens, my discovery was too late.

Just like that snake, the evil serpent, Satan, will take his time stalking his prey, testing each link in the fence, looking for weaknesses. If he finds a hole, the entire fence is rendered ineffective in keeping him out. It's just as useless as if there were no fence to begin with. Our fences must be secure to be effective, and one way that we can help secure the barrier is through family devotions.

> The "Prince of Preachers," C.H. Spurgeon, once said, "If we want to bring up a godly family, who shall be a seed to serve God when our heads are under the clods of the valley, let us seek to train them up in the fear of God by meeting together as a family for worship."[13]

Every family represented in my study had one thing in common: they felt a great need for the Word of God. In fact, the Bible was the heart of these godly families. Though they were not perfect, they made their decisions based on the question, "What would God want me to do?" They discovered what God said in His Word and endeavored to implement its principles in their daily lives.

David, who was raised on the mission field and then himself became a missionary, felt that family devotions was one of the most important things his parents did which pointed him in the direction of serving the Lord. "Family devotions greatly influenced my life," he explained. "Sometimes we got interrupted, and maybe on a rare occasion we forgot or something, but we would get back to it. It was very important to my family."

Crystal, another missionary's daughter, told how family devotions opened the door for her to ask her parents some very important questions. "When I was 5," she said, "I remember that I got baptized, but as I got older and thought about it, I realized I didn't really remember actually asking God to save me then. By the time I was 12, I began to have some serious doubts about whether or not I was truly born-again. During devotions, however, I was able to talk to Dad, and I thank the Lord I got peace right then."

Neil, the son of a former up-and-coming-country music singer, remembers his family's Bible time. "Many topics which were brought up during family devotions seemed to help us kids talk about things that were not normally brought up. We had some of the best discussions. It helped me solidify what I believed and why." For Neil, Crystal, David and many others, spending time with God as a family was an important part of growing up.

The importance of having regular family devotions cannot be overstated. It takes only a light perusal of the Word of God to see that it is imperative for the parents, particularly the fathers, to take it upon themselves to teach their children the Word of God.

> . . . the father to the children shall make known thy truth. (Isaiah 38:19)

> I will open my mouth in a parable: I will utter dark sayings of old: Which we have heard and known, and our fathers have told us. We will not hide them from their children, shewing to the generation to come the praises of the LORD, and his strength, and his wonderful works that he hath done. (Psalm 78:2-4)

For these families, the phrase "The family that prays together, stays together" was not just a plaque on their wall; it was a way of life. "I knew my mom was always there to pray with me," Steve explained. "Even now, Mom and Dad have a big part in our lives. They are concerned about me and seek to keep me close to them and close to the Lord."

As a family, you may not have regular Bible time with God. But that doesn't mean all is lost. There were a few that did not have devotions regularly growing up. However, it was something they wished they had done. Rachel said, "Looking back, I would say that I wish Mom and Dad had taken more time for family devotions, to set that habit into my life when I was younger."

Arianna echoed a similar concern. "We rarely had family devotions growing up," she told me. "That's something I would really like to do when the Lord gives my husband and me children of our own."

So, if you don't have a time every day when you spend time in the Word of God as a family, it's not too late to start! It doesn't matter where; you could start in Genesis, or Revelation (though I don't recommend starting at Revelation for beginners!). You could take thirty minutes, or you could take ten. You may have had family devotions before but got sidetracked. It hardly matters; today is a new day – start anew and afresh!

All that matters is that you DO IT. Check your barrier; look for holes or breaks. Do whatever you can to seal the fence. My conclusion is that, though having family devotions does not *guarantee* success, it definitely can't help but help.

And for me, I need all the help I can get!

Cementing the Barrier: Instructing Young People with a Christian World View

Martin Luther said, "I'm afraid that the schools will prove the very gates of hell, unless they diligently labor in explaining the Holy Scriptures and engraving them in the heart of youth." Luther believed in the importance of training children in the Word of God.

Similarly, the vast majority of our respondents had some sort of a Christian education, whether it was home schooling or attending a Christian school. Less than one eighth of our respondents attended public school, while an overwhelming 88% had a decidedly Christian education.

The Bible says in Deuteronomy 6:6-8, "And these words, which I command Thee this day, shall be in thine heart: And thou shalt teach them diligently unto thy children, and shalt talk of them when Thou sittest in thine house, and when Thou walkest by the way, and when Thou liest down, and when Thou risest up."

Passing on Biblical values to the next generation is not only an act of obedience to God's clear commands to parents, but it is extremely important to the outcome of our child raising as well. Current statistics, however, show us that passing on the torch to the next generation is generally not accomplished in our culture. Consider the differences between home school graduates and their public school counterparts:

> By the time your children graduate from school, how many of them will believe in Jesus?
>
> Homeschooled: 94%
>
> Public Schooled: 15%
>
> 94% of homeschoolers keep the faith and 93% continue to attend church after the high school years. But a shocking 75% to 85% of Christian children sent to public school drop out of church, and do not hold a Christian worldview after high school graduation.[14]

Though statistics regarding the beliefs of Christian school graduates are currently unavailable, I feel it is very likely that your average Christian school graduate is somewhere in the middle.

Our respondents' parents felt that a Christian education was important enough for them to make tremendous sacrifices. They made sure their children got a quality education, while at the same time preserving the priority of serving the Lord in the minds of their children. Maintaining involvement was significant to them as well, understanding that a Christian education is no substitute for parental participation in the lives of the young people, but a wonderful addition to it.

The research shows that a Christian education is markedly better than government education for producing young people who love and serve the Lord. With that understood, only one of those I interviewed did or are planning to send their children to public school. The remaining 98%, even those who attended government schools, are now sending their own children to Christian school or even educating them at home. They fully understand that the current educational system is not something to which they want their children exposed.

Having an unapologetically Christian education is another way to cement the barrier, and help our children become LIONPROOF.

ENTERTAINMENT

There are many things in life that are not wrong to use. But many *good* things can be used to a *bad* end thus destroying both the user and those around him. A good example of this is medicine: various medications are highly beneficial, but they can also be abused.

One day not long ago, I received a frantic call from a friend. "Please pray for my teenage daughter; she took an entire bottle of Tylenol PM, and she's in the hospital!" After a few questions, I found out that this young lady had actually tried to commit suicide. How? By taking way too much of a good thing. She used Tylenol PM for the wrong reasons, and almost ruined her liver!

Overuse of a good thing turns it into a bad thing. Too much soda is another illustration of this point. We love that yummy, sweet drink, but if we drink too much of it, it can wreak havoc on your body's delicate balance, making us feel terrible. Even honey, that wonderful natural sweetener, is to be taken in moderation. The Bible says, "It is not good to eat much honey" (Proverbs 25:27a)

That is not to say that all sin is merely an overuse of something; that would be a gross oversimplification. Sin is transgression of God's law, as we go our own way and do our own will instead of God's. But when we talk about entertainment, even some good things can lead to sin when we misuse them. For example, if I use a chair to try to reach the top shelf, it would be dangerous. By using the chair for something other than sitting, I put myself into a hazardous position, and increase the likelihood that I will get hurt.

The same is true with entertainment. Using the Internet for research is a good thing, but using the Internet for entertainment can be morally very dangerous. Pornography, for instance, is much more readily available on the internet than ever before. Even the new so-called "mommy porn," erotica, is spreading like a bad case of poison oak.

There are three things parents must watch out for concerning entertainment: 1) Its moral effects, 2) its spiritual effects, and 3) overuse. Because of this, wise parents will be careful about what their children watch or play and how much.

Study after study has shown that violent media can have serious detrimental effects on children, even causing Post Traumatic Stress Disorder after only one exposure. Even advertising is a concern, since very young children are unable to see the persuasive objective.[15]There are also physical concerns such as: increased obesity, greater likelihood of smoking, less sleep, and increased risk of ADHD.[16]

If media can have a detrimental effect physically and psychologically, we must also realize that there is very likely a detrimental effect morally and spiritually.

Over the years, Hollywood has undermined morality and mocked Christianity. An adult may be able to discern and choose Biblical values anyway, but a young child is rarely able to. Morally and spiritually, concerned parents must be wise, informed, and willing to get involved.

Some forms of entertainment are constructive and fun, but even those can be potentially harmful when used too much. There are also some forms of entertainment that are contraband, or strictly forbidden. These are the forms of recreation that should not be used at all; they are HIGHLY DANGEROUS!

So, we see that entertainment falls into these categories:

Types of Entertainment	General effect	Effects on the family	Examples
Acceptable Entertainment	Helpful	Brings people together Makes people happier	board games, outdoor family fun, occasional edifying and educational electronic media
Overused Entertainment	Potentially harmful	May create schisms in the family May tend to cause bickering among family members, grumpiness and moodiness	*constant* playing of board games, electronic media daily for extended periods of time, etc.
Misused Entertainment	Dangerous	Takes a good thing and uses it for an alternate purpose	using videos for a babysitter, etc.
		Feeds selfishness	"get those little brats out of my hair for a bit!" Using media alone as an "out;" no other relaxing pursuits

Types of Entertainment	General effect	Effects on the family	Examples
Contraband Entertainment	Destructive	Completely selfish; gives individuals over to lustful desires and poor moral judgments; causes emotional unhappiness, destroys family unity, often causes family breakups	pornography, alcohol, gambling, etc.

Every family draws their line somewhere regarding entertainment. Most families draw their line by default: whatever is convenient at the time. However, the parents of our respondents drew their lines intentionally— preventatively, carefully, and prayerfully. They decided ahead of time and through much thought, prayer and study what they would do (and *not* do) for entertainment.

Their testimonies are consistent: entertainment was limited.

These families understood the need to monitor entertainment in the home. By contrast, another study of the Christian community by George Barna found that, "the media monitoring process in the household was indistinguishable from the approach taken by parents who are not born-again."[17]In other words, the rules concerning entertainment—what TV shows and movies to watch, how much to watch, what computer games to play, etc. —are no different than your average American household.

However, 100% of the people who responded to my survey had limits on their entertainment. Several (52%) were raised without any TV at all, while the rest (48%) had limits on the amount and the kinds of TV they could watch. Videos, computer games, and internet use were the same story: *limited.*

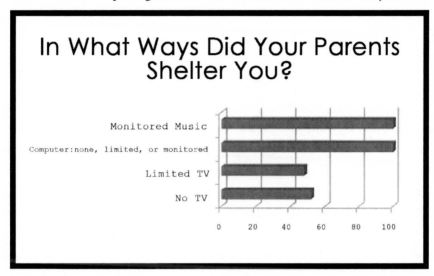

"Yes, I was sheltered, Steve explained."My parents kept me away from some people, they limited TV, videos, media outlets, and controlled the music I listened to. They guided me through my growing-up years, and I know it really helped me."

Brittany's youth pastor husband Tim, agreed. "It was good for me that I was sheltered," he said. "I was looking to get into trouble but couldn't find it. The Lord was good to me."

Interestingly, not one person I talked to seemed bothered by such restrictions. They seemed to understand that it is a normal part of being a servant of God. Either the parents adequately explained their reasoning, or the young people came to understand on their own.

This brings up another excellent point, and that is that many of my respondents spoke of the need for parents to communicate the *reasons* behind their rules. We'll discuss that point more in Chapter 11: Navigating the Teen Years.

These numbers tell a huge story, and may help explain why so many of these second-generation Christians have chosen to embrace the values of their parents. When combined with the consistent example of godly parents, creating a wholesome atmosphere in the home is perhaps one of the most significant differences between your average "Christian" home and the *godly* homes of our faithful respondents.

FRIENDS

The third category of sheltering lies in the area of friendships. Friends are a powerful influence for good or for evil. In the Bible, David's friend Jonathan was a companion who encouraged him in the Lord. By contrast, David's son Amnon had a sneaky, conniving friend named Jonadab who advised him to rape his half-sister, Tamar. Amnon didn't plan such a scheme his own; he had the influence of a wicked friend, and he followed his friend's advice.

Some studies show, in fact, that friends are the greatest influence for wrong. A recent study done by Students Against Drunk Driving and Liberty Mutual found that "Close friends are teens' number one influence when making destructive decisions."[18]

My interviews revealed not only why many second generation Christians are serving the Lord, but why many of their peers *are not*. Because they grew up together, it was easy for those I interviewed to see where their friends made bad choices. Many times, these bad choices involved choosing the wrong friends.

"I have two older sisters; one serving God and one out of church," Robbie said. "The one who is out of church had friends she shouldn't have had, who ended up turning her heart away from the Lord. Now she has bitterness against herself because of it—bitterness because she disappointed Mom and Dad, and bitterness because she doesn't do what she knows she's supposed to do"

By contrast, I noticed that 99% of my respondents told how their parents shielded them from friends who would turn them away from God. In fact, it was often the very first thing they said when asked whether their parents sheltered them.

"Dad was very strict on who I was allowed to be friends with," Susan explained. "He didn't want me to be friends with just anybody. I guess he could see who was a good influence and who wasn't. He would tell me, 'You can be nice to her, but you're not going to get close to her.' I know it was for my good, because many of those 'friends' are not serving the Lord now."

Steve agreed. "I didn't have many friends, because my dad worked at a boys' home. Though I lived there, wasn't allowed to get close to the boys in the home. I didn't need the friendship of those boys."

These godly parents carefully monitored the relationships of their young people. May we all learn from their success and do the same.

MUSIC

Perhaps one of the most formative influences of a young person's mind and character is the kind of music to which they listen. Not surprisingly, every one of our second generation respondents were limited as to the kind of music to which they were exposed. Most of them specified that rock, hip-hop, rap, pop, and jazz music were simply not allowed in their home.

I spoke with Sheila, a delightful mother of four, as we sat in her backyard watching a river flow by. Her cheerful attitude was quite contagious. She chuckled softly and said, "It's kinda funny now, thinking back on it. My parents were always accused of being too strict, too harsh, having too high standards, etc. But that was from people who were looking in, not those in our home. We were all so happy, and we had a lot of leeway." Smiling, she continued, "Now, my parents are the only ones I know who still have the same standards that they had before AND have all their six children in the ministry . . . as for music, it was a conservative Christian radio station, or no music at all."

That's just one of the many examples I could give. Still, several of my interviewees told how music played a part in their temporary lapse into rebellion. Though they didn't go far into worldliness and never really got out of church, it was far enough for them to have problems.

Robbie was one of those young teens. "I guess as I became a teenager, I got curious about music, and I began listening to rock," he said. "When I was part of a big football program at the Christian school, it was just the thing to do, and I got sucked into it. I began listening to rock music, and I became more and more rebellious. It led me down the wrong path for a little while, but God was good to me, and brought me back before I got too far."

Tim also spoke candidly about his short foray into rebellion, "While I was visiting a Christian college, I realized it was my music that was holding me back from serving God. He convicted me, and got me pointed back in the right direction."

It is not surprising to see why the parents of these people were careful about the music that came into their homes.

In his highly informative, thoroughly researched and documented book titled <u>Media Violence and Children</u>, Douglas Gentile shows how music is an integral part in young peoples' lives. From his research, he has found:

- Young people spend almost as much time listening to music as watching TV (twenty-one hours per week, and twenty-five hours per week, respectively).

- Young people would choose music over TV if stranded on a desert isle.

- Young people often get their values from music.

- The type of music one listens to helps define oneself and one's in-group.[19]

As Christian parents, our desire is that our young people will define themselves as followers of Jesus Christ, not followers of rock stars, Hollywood idols, or MTV. When they define themselves as godly Christians and seek to associate with those of the same group, a very large part of the battle is won.

And then, we learn that hard rock music can even be physically dangerous, according to an experiment performed by student David Merrell in Virginia in 1997. Groups of mice listened to classical music, hard rock, or no music at all. The classical mice became faster in running the maze, whereas the hard rock mice became slower. The student performing the study stated, "I had to cut my project short because all the hard-rock mice killed each other. . . . None of the classical mice did that." In a second experiment, David kept the mice in individual cages so they wouldn't harm each other. Still, the hard rock music mice had more and more trouble running through their maze.[20]

Many people believe "but it's not the music itself, it's the lyrics that cause all the troubles." It can be easily noted, however, that mice cannot understand lyrics; they simply feel the music itself. The research results are in: a 1991 study cited by Gentile proved that heavy metal music had disturbing and aggressive undertones, **regardless of the lyrics.**

The somewhat surprising result was that it did not matter whether participants heard sexually violent heavy metal or Christian heavy metal. Relative to classical music, exposure to either type of music produced more negative attitudes toward women. In other words, the lyrics did not make a difference, but the heavy metal musical form did.[21]

Brittany, whom we met earlier, is perhaps one of the most impressive respondents to my survey. Her father, Jeff, is currently a music and choir director at a large church in a northern city, and *his* father was also a music director at another church in the Midwest. Brittany is highly active in the music ministry of her church, along with both her brothers in their respective churches. In fact, my delightful interview with Brittany revealed that her great-grandfather wrote a very famous hymn in the mid-1800s.

What does all this mean to you and me? It means that good music choices are highly influential to the next generation. This family is a pristine example of passing down godly values, serving the Lord with their talents, and consistently living for God generation after generation. It all started over a hundred years ago when one man trusted Christ as his Savior and turned from worldly music to music that honors Christ. He filled his life and soul with godly music, and from his pen and heart flowed one of the most beloved hymns of all time. And from the musical talents of his descendants, many thousands have been blessed and encouraged to live for God.

Why did these parents feel the need to shelter their children so? The answer lies in Bible principles, upon which their very lives are founded. Separation from the world is an extremely important dynamic to preserve a biblical world view for the next generation.

> Be ye not unequally yoked together with unbelievers: for what fellowship hath righteousness with unrighteousness? and what communion hath light with darkness? And what concord hath Christ with Belial? or what part hath he that believeth with an infidel? And what agreement hath the temple of God with idols? for ye are the temple of the living God; as God hath said, I will dwell in them, and walk in them; and I will be their God, and they shall be my people. Wherefore come out from among them, and be ye separate, saith the Lord, and touch not the unclean thing; and I will receive you, And will be a Father unto you, and ye shall be my sons and daughters, saith the Lord Almighty. Having therefore

these promises, dearly beloved, let us cleanse ourselves from all filthiness of the flesh and spirit, perfecting holiness in the fear of God. (2 Corinthians 7:14-8:1)

Here's how it works:

My family lives in a bus-converted-motor home, and my husband does his own maintenance. Though he saves money by being a Do-It-Yourself guy, he always emerges from the engine compartment looking like he's fallen into an oil spill. I don't mind if he's in his work clothes, but if he's wearing his best white shirt and red silk tie, he'd better stay away from the greasy areas. Separation from the engine compartment is important if he wants to keep clean . . . and make me happy.

The same way, separation from the world keeps us from getting dirty! It doesn't make us any better than anyone else; it merely makes us cleaner and safer, and the Lord can use us more.

> But in a great house there are not only vessels of gold and of silver, but also of wood and of earth; and some to honour, and some to dishonour. If a man therefore purge himself from these, he shall be a vessel unto honour, sanctified, and meet for the master's use, and prepared unto every good work. Flee also youthful lusts: but follow righteousness, faith, charity, peace, with them that call on the Lord out of a pure heart. (2 Timothy 2:20-22)

Sheltering is an important part of raising godly children. It provides a solid basis upon which godly worldviews may be established, and right living may be embraced. The fact that these people were carefully and prayerfully sheltered gives evidence to the effectiveness of keeping children unspotted by the world.

"In my opinion," Julia explained, "some may not be sheltering their kids enough from harmful influences: TV and friends that are a bad influence, for example. I even think that nowadays, parents need to consider protecting their children from internet social networking." Leaning toward me, she said earnestly, "Sheltering the kids is VERY important. I cannot stress enough how essential it is. For me, I feel it made a big difference in my life."

These parents did not want their children to live in a world of sex, drugs, crime, and heartache. They understood that, in order to "Lionproof" their children, they needed to raise them differently from others, and to keep them unspotted from the world. No matter what criticism they received from others, they did what they felt was right to do. Because of their insistence on following what God impressed upon their hearts, their children kept from the claws of the Devil.

DON'T STOP READING...

I hasten to add here a warning to those of you who wish to stop reading right here. You've been supplied with all your tools to build your barriers and keep your children from the world. And it is true that they must be sheltered. However, understand that it is very easy to fall into the trap that many good parents fall into, and that is the tendency to pull the barriers so tightly that they choke a young person and stifle his ability to interact with others. Be careful; if you create a cloistered environment, it is quite possible that your dear sheltered young person may find a break in the hedge someday and decide to make a run for it.

If he does, he plays right into the Devil's paws. You can be sure that the hungry lion will be waiting for him when he, with eyes round with bewilderment, comes out of his safe haven. He is right where Satan wants him.

But you will not shelter your child without telling him why, or hold onto him too long, or for the wrong reasons, because you will have kept on reading and learned what successful parents have done through the teenage years.

LIONPROOF STRATEGY #5:
BUILD A BARRICADE!

PREPARING YOUR DEFENSE

1. In your opinion, what are the avenues Satan can use to influence people? Do young people have a different set of influences than older ones?

2. Take some time to evaluate the following Scriptures: 1 Timothy 3:15; Psalm 92:12-13; 1 Corinthians 14:12. How important is church to you?

3. There are plenty of materials available to help with Family Devotions if you feel inadequate. Nothing takes the place of some heartfelt instruction by Dad, however simple it may be.

4. Think about the friends you had when you were young. Briefly make a list of them, and write beside each one whether their influence in your life was good or bad. Think carefully about why they were so influential.

Next, make a list of your children, and beside them, write the names of their friends. Are those friends a good influence on them or a bad influence? Determine some steps to take to guide your child into making good choices in his friendships.

ASSIGNMENT:

1. If you do not already have Family Devotions, go ahead and start! It doesn't have to be long or fancy—just getting the family together, reading the Bible, and praying together can make a tremendous difference! Date Family Devotions started:_____

2. As a couple, pray seriously about the modes of sheltering that the Lord would want you to have. As God leads, begin making some changes—with a joyful attitude, knowing that you're doing the right thing!

    Replace any activity that you are dropping with a good alternative, preferably with some activity that will bind you together as a family.

3. Have a brainstorming session to come up with a list of fun things your kids can do. You may even want them to help you out! Perhaps you need to invest in some board games or sports equipment.

THOUGHT QUESTIONS for Chapter 7:

1. In your opinion, what really is Biblical correction?

2. How does Biblical correction affect children who grow up in Christian homes?

3. What are some ways you think people wrong their children by either over-correcting or under-correcting?

CHAPTER 7:
THE NECESSARY ART OF LOVING CORRECTION

"Go where you may, you will find no rest except in humble obedience to the rule of authority". —Thomas a Kempis, Imitation of Christ

"Correct thy son, and he shall give thee rest; yea, he shall give delight unto thy soul."
Proverbs 29:17

Have you ever wondered how successful parents taught their children the difference betweenright and wrong? Did they use corporal punishment, and if so, was it abusive? Did it harm their children?

Perhaps you have skipped the rest of the book and come directly to this chapter, just to see what I'm going to say. If you are one of those folks, then you will not see the context of discipline. Be advised that, before you jump to any conclusions, you should carefully read the rest of the book.

I understand that there is a lot of discussion about the negative side of this issue, but if you could do what I have done, if you could talk at length to dozens of godly, happy, well-adjusted adults and ask them some very specific questions about their childhoods, you would develop a picture of a loving home, with carefully and lovingly administered correction. You would see that their home is happy because the children learn to obey, and ultimately because the parents obeyed the Word of God by training their children carefully. You would see a home where the kids go to bed without a struggle, the parents devotedly care for the children, and the young people are happy and pleasant.

It is this picture I want you to have in your mind as you read this chapter. I'm not talking about robots; I'm talking about young people who understand their boundaries and have joyfully embraced the place God has for them. These people know that one of Satan's big strategies is to magnify limitations, thereby creating discontent. But these young folks have chosen to focus instead on the possibilities of serving the Lord. Though perhaps they didn't understand it at the time, they eventually comprehended and benefitted by the discipline they received as children.

At first, I wrestled with this chapter, but since 100% of my respondents told me that they received discipline as a youngster, I need to talk about it. I feel that the importance of early discipline cannot be overstated.

In this chapter we will learn why some discipline is completely ineffective, what kind of correction really works, why it works, and the real secret to effective discipline.

Let me start by saying that there is a way to discipline that is actually harmful rather than helpful. I call this:

Selfish Discipline

There were a very few that told of extremes in discipline. Larry, an older pastor in a mid western town, told me how different his mother's discipline was than his father's. "I didn't get many whippings from Dad, but when I did, it was a good one. But Mom was different. She was very impatient and yelled a lot. She was even what I would consider abusive. She beat us with anything she could get a hold of and on any part of the body. My younger brother picked up on Mom's bitter spirit, and now he's a sour person."

Larry understood why his father disciplined him, but his mother's irritation could only be interpreted as selfishness. The children reacted to her selfishness and frustration, and it created bitterness.

In Selfish Discipline:

1. The goal of the parent is his or her own comfort

2. Punishment is performed out of frustration and anger

3. The parent merely bullies a young person into submission "because I said so!"

4. Discipline is not connected in any way with the crime committed.

Larry's brother still feels the effects of his mother's abuse. As a middle-aged man, he is an alcoholic who doesn't like anybody, and I suspect that few people like him either.

"Selfish Discipline is not Biblical discipline! *It has never produced happy, productive, and godly young people, and never will.* Not surprisingly, this is not the way most of my godly second-generation respondents were raised.

> *"Selfishness is basically the root of all sin and unhappiness. The Scriptures speak over and over again on the evils of selfishness. Selfishness is not happiness and will never bring happiness."*
> ~Cael Sanderson,

Now, let's turn away from Larry and look at the rest of my respondents.

Introducing Loving Correction

Taking a broader view, we realize that corporal punishment is just one method of negative reinforcement in the whole process of training a child in the way he should go. (See Proverbs 22:6) Just as a battery has both positive and negative poles, so also child training requires both positive and negative reinforcement.

These parents of the second generation respondents used what I call "Loving Correction." When a child was doing something he wasn't supposed to, or headed in a wrong direction, the parent lovingly directed the child back into the right way. It was not discipline—punishing for wrong—but it was correction—bringing back into line with right.

There are many ways this was accomplished:

When the Permanent Way Inspector arrived at the camp where the lions had been raiding, he surveyed the frightened crew, or what was left of them, with consternation. "What's the matter with your coolies, Patterson?" he sneered. "Are they a bunch of women that they are so frightened by these rumors?"

Patterson glared hard at the man, then raised an eyebrow and replied evenly, "Unless you shelter yourself before dusk every night, you may just have one of those 'rumors' find you. I suggest you take heed to our warnings and retire early."

Only a few nights later, the remaining lion was on the prowl once more. He soon found something promising: a small wooden shelter occupied by the Permanent Way Inspector. Making his way up the steps, he prowled around, but not finding a way in, the lion went back down the steps and pounced on some goats. The Inspector listened with horror as his animals were consumed right below his home.

- Praise, which is positive reinforcement.

- Reproof, which is instruction in the way of life.

- Restrictions, which help a child understand that there really are limits in life. One young man, Micah, grinned as he said, "It's very effective when a young man has his car taken away for a bit. I had that happen a lot."

- Finally, there is corporal punishment, the ultimate negative reinforcement.

The goal of Loving Correction is to benefit of the young people, not to make the parents look good. Loving Correction directs the young person in the way of maturity, duty, and responsibility rather than feeding their self-will. It points them to the happy path of success through good character.

Loving Correction is what almost all of my interviewees experienced. In fact, ninety-six percent of them reported that they were disciplined by their parents:

1. **Only** when necessary

"I didn't get many spankings growing up," Abby explained thoughtfully. "It's not that I was perfect or anything, I just never wanted to disappoint my parents."

2. **Rarely** in anger

I talked to Todd, a steady young pastor's son, after church one Sunday in southern

California. He spoke openly about his father's very effective discipline. "I can't think of a time my parents got angry. There were times Dad pulled me aside and talked to me, but he never yelled at me."

Though some reported that their parents occasionally got angry, they explained that it was rare. Jamie was one of those people. "My dad sometimes got angry," she said. "But he seemed to keep the line and not sin . . . preparing for trips, he would sometimes get uptight. Mostly, though, there were not a lot of angry outbursts."

3. **Equal** in proportion to the crimes committed

Sheila said meditatively, "We were never abused. Spankings were rare and consisted of usually about three to five licks, depending on the crime. Most often, though, there was a very stern rebuke."

4. With a goal of **Gradual training** in the habit of obedience

Tracy, a pastor's daughter who is now a missionary's wife, told me about the results of her early training in the habit of obedience. "We had many rules, very strictly enforced," she said. Eventually, the effect of such discipline became evident. "If I was told to take out the trash and clean the bedroom, I would never think twice about doing it in the exact manner I was told."

5. **Gradually enlisting** the young person's will to service and submission . . . "because it is right."

Jay, who was quite a handful as a youngster, said, "I didn't always like what my folks did, but I eventually understood what they were trying to teach me."

6. **Decisively** when the child is rebellious

Having been a rebellious teen himself, Robbie's experience and wisdom are very helpful to us. "I started going down the wrong path with a bunch of friends," he told me, "and I ended up hurting my dad's heart. My dad dealt pretty harshly with me, but I deserved it. It broke my heart to realize that I had hurt my dad. I feared Dad, and it became a fear of God. At that point, God became very REAL in my life, and I decided I wanted to serve God on my own."

His dad dealt quickly, strongly, and decisively with his son's rebellion.
It became the turning point in Robbie's life.

It is hard sometimes for us as parents to realize just how important little things are to a child. Little concessions we make, little allowances for sin, and little occasions of permitting their bad attitudes can grow into glaring deficiencies in their character, and ultimately a lack of concern for spiritual things, which can result in rebellion.

The importance of Early Loving Correction

Good character—those qualities of caring for others, being responsible, doing one's duty, protecting those less fortunate, being considerate and kind—is at a premium these days. Though it may seem rare to find people with these qualities, they are present in large quantities among my second-generation respondents. These are folks who go the second mile to help someone, pull their share of the load and then some, and are patient and gentle in their dealings with others. Why? Because these qualities were instilled into them from the time they were born.

Undoubtedly, the parents of these young people understood the need to develop character early. Good habits will carry a person to success, and the satisfaction of a job well done brings its own reward. Therefore, the first step in developing a happy adult lies in raising responsible and mature young people—people with character.

Not only is Angela a Christian School teacher, but she is also a sixth generation Christian. Good habits were ingrained into her and her sisters while they were quite young. "I was spanked—only if I did something wrong—until I was eleven years old," she said earnestly. "My dad felt that if you disciplined early and correctly, you wouldn't have to do it when the children were older. There was no grounding—we just obeyed. Sometimes we might 'earn' extra chores, though." Those "extra chores" went a long way in helping them develop maturity.

Another thing the parents of these second-generation Christians worked to instill was a good attitude. They understood that a person's attitude determines their "altitude", or how far they can go. While encouraging their children to have good attitudes, they also discouraged bad ones. Arianna said, "My father disciplined us for attitude trouble. He said, 'That's a bad attitude, and I don't want to see it.'"

Knowing Arianna as I do, I can attest that her father's wisdom and teaching went a long way to benefitting her life! Her joyful attitude as an adult is a blessing to everyone.

Loving Correction goes hand-in-hand with the next, but probably the most important, point. It is:

The Secret to Effective Correction

When we converted our first bus into a motor home, my husband wanted a little more head room on the inside, so he decided to add eight inches to the height of the roof. To do that, he literally cut the entire bus horizontally into two pieces right above the windows, and then used jacks to raise the roof bit by bit. The newly created gap in the sides was filled in with sheets of metal, but the slanted front cap above the windshield was another story. For that, he used fiberglass. He mixed two chemicals, resin and hardener, in a paint trough, and dipped the fiberglass mat into it, thoroughly soaking it. Then he put the mat onto the frame he had built into that eight inch space, covering it completely. The addition of the hardener did just that – it hardened the fiberglass mat, and turned it from a flexible fabric into a strong but lightweight plastic. "Without the hardener," my fix-it-all husband tells me, "the whole process is wasted. The resin looks, smells, and feels the same without the hardener, but it never turns into what you want. We needed to add the proper second chemical. The hardener 'magically' turns it into super-strong plastic."

Similarly, my second-generation respondents spoke freely about the most important ingredient in child training, without which the whole process is wasted. In fact, it is so effective, it combines with and magnifies the effect of any kind of discipline which a parent uses. What is this catalyst?

It is the all-important *relationship.*

Nothing is more important to your young person than his relationship with you! Perhaps you've heard the saying, "Rules without relationship breed rebellion."

Brittany put it this way, "There was not much corporal punishment when we got older. If anything happened, we got privileges taken away. Basically, we never wanted to disappoint Mom and Dad. My brother and I talked about whether or not to do wrong, but we always decided that the consequences for doing something we weren't supposed to do weren't worth the 'fun' of doing wrong. Our parents had our hearts from a young age."

Lena is a young home school graduate who now works at an accounting office in Indiana. She said, "I had a close relationship with my mom, and a break in that relationship was punishment enough."

Just like resin is not effective without the hardener, so discipline—in *any* form —is not effective without a good relationship.

The Positive Effects of Loving Correction

> *"Now no chastening for the present seemeth to be joyous, but grievous: nevertheless afterward it yieldeth the peaceable fruit of righteousness unto them which are exercised thereby." (Hebrews 12:11)*

In the world of the brown bear, there are plenty of things for new cubs to learn: how to protect themselves, how to gather food, and how to keep away from dangers. The cubs spend lots of times playing with each other. Not all is fun and games for a cub, however.

No one knows what the brown cub did to bring on his mother's discipline in March 2012 at the Simferopol Zoo in the Ukraine, but it's fairly certain that he will never do it again. A series of pictures shows the mother bear grabbing her cub by the scruff of the neck and tossing him up in the air, then roaring menacingly at him as he flattens himself in fear against the wall. Finally, when he comes back with his head down, she draws him close and gives him a nice big bear hug! All is forgiven and a big lesson is learned.[22]

Many people feel that corporal punishment is completely ineffective. My respondents, however, did not feel that way; in fact, they eventually learned some very important lessons through discipline

"I remember my parents making rules," Suzanna told me, "and I cried when I was disciplined. But looking back now, I realize they had a reason. There were things I couldn't see but they could."

Joanne explained, "We were spanked when we were little. Not very often, but we knew it was the ultimate end. We never got grounded much. When we stepped out of line, they (Mom and Dad) would talk to us. Once I got old enough, I didn't often go against their word."

Joanne, like many others, shows us that early and consistent Loving Correction produces secure young people who know they are loved, understand their boundaries, and are ready to be useful to others by living unselfish lives.

Also, early and consistent Loving Correction often paves the way for a close relationship with the Lord. I was riveted by the testimony of Tracy, who I quoted earlier. Here is the rest of her statement: "If I was told to take out the trash and clean the bedroom, I would never think twice about doing it in the exact manner I was told. That's why I never question the Lord. I never questioned my parents, and I never question the Lord."

Greg is a young assistant pastor who also is a successful entrepreneur. Though he is still in his mid-twenties, his faithfulness and thoroughness on the job are building a strong reputation, and he finds himself busier than ever. Not surprisingly, he is a man of few words. "We feared Dad," Greg explained, "and therefore feared God."

Greg realizes that a child will often think of God the same way he thinks of a parent. If a child loves, respects, and obeys his parents, it becomes so much easier to transfer that heart of dedication to the Lord. Obedience is an important lesson Greg is trying to teach his two young children, ages one and three.

In our quest to pass on our values to the next generation, we should never underestimate the value of Loving Correction. It is not abuse, nor is it bullying. It is perhaps one of the most gentle and caring ways of showing someone the difference between right and wrong, and starting them on their way to a joyous life. To care for children is to guide them in the way of responsibility and nobility, duty and selflessness, strength and virtue.

****

Standing at the top of the stairs of the wedding altar, my son's eyes filled with tears as his bride came down the aisle. The fact that they both were desperately in love was obvious to everyone, but few people knew what I knew about my son.

Sitting in the pew during the ceremony, my mind went back to those days of his childhood, years before. Though perhaps he hadn't always had such a tender heart, my son became sensitive to the Lord after he gave his heart to Christ. He was not the perfect child, but he had a desire to obey.

When he was just a little fellow, my boy was just like any other young, energetic boy, who loved to romp in the woods. Knowing how destructive little boys can be sometimes, my husband warned him, "Son, don't go running like a crazy man through the forest breaking up trees. You don't want to just destroy things just because they're there."

Like a shot, he was off, running through the woods, having a great time. After a while, he came back and told us, "Dad, I know you told me not to go breaking trees. I just wanted to let you know that I was running, and I accidently bumped into one of them and broke it off. I'm sorry."

My Beloved was tempted to dismiss his confession as silly, but he realized that our son was telling us, out of the softness of his heart, that he realized he had inadvertently done something which he was told not to do. Perhaps he was being hyper-obedient, but that was a really good sign: his conscience was tender and used to obeying.

We came to value his tender conscience. We found that, as he grew older, he could be trusted to be forthright and true to his integrity.

When he became a young man, this son seemed genuinely concerned about doing what he was supposed to do. He asked many questions. "What do you think about this, Dad? What about that? Is this ok?" Through a good relationship, early loving correction, and approachability, he was forming his own values.

Not long before the wedding, he had gotten a job on a construction crew, and was teased mercilessly because he is not immoral or loose like most young men today. He took it good-naturedly, knowing that it is unusual for a man in his mid-twenties to be morally pure. Now the Lord was blessing him with a beautiful wife who loved him dearly.

I tried in vain to blink back the tears as my son sang to his sweetheart a beautiful song of love, commitment, and loyalty. Like a lightning bolt, I realized that because he learned to obey us when he was young, he learned to obey the Lord when he got older. Careful, early, loving correction brought him to the marriage altar in love with his wife, and in love with the Lord—pure, holy, and blameless.

The beauty of such dedicated love and obedience is virtually inexpressible.

LIONPROOF STRATEGY #6:
EMPLOY LOVING CORRECTION!

PREPARING YOUR DEFENSE:

1. A proper understanding of how Loving Correction applies to you begins with a proper understanding of your own childhood. Think back to the discipline, or perhaps correction, you received as a child. Did it help you or harm you? Most likely, you already innately shy away from something you feel was bad for you as a child. Perhaps your parents went overboard on the area of discipline, so you tend to go overboard the other direction, trying not to repeat the same mistake. Be careful! Herein lies the great deception: By throwing away correction altogether, you may very well leave your children exposed to the paws of the waiting lion. Be courageous enough to lay out your heart before the Lord and ask Him to help you become effective in this area as a parent. Forgive the errors of those who have wronged you, move on, and resolve to do better.

2. Understanding that successful parents employ Loving Correction, consider the steps you will take to utilize the same. Take into account the importance of consistency – if you make a rule and punish for it once, you must be willing to punish for it *every time*.

3. Once you establish a rule, expect your young people to wait awhile, then try to do what you tell them not to do. Not necessarily out of an evil heart, but just because they would prefer doing things their own way. Here's where the watchful eye of the diligent parent comes in—particularly the mother since she is typically around the children more than the father. Just because a certain length of time elapses before an infringement of the rule doesn't mean the coast is clear. "Be thou diligent to know the state of thy flocks, and look well to thy herds" (Proverbs 27:23).

4. Think of the past. Ask yourself, "Have I meant what I said? Have the kids been told something that I've not carried through with, whether it was a promise of reward or of punishment? Have I ever said, 'If you do this (something

good,) I'll take you to ___" but not followed through? Conversely, have I ever threatened punishment but didn't follow through?"

5. Think of the present. Ask yourself when the urge arises to promise either a punishment or a reward, "Do I really mean this? Am I willing to follow through with it, even if it is inconvenient or costly to me? Am I willing to take a temporary loss to get a permanent gain?"

6. Think of the children. Take a young person aside and talk to them, saying, "God's been speaking to us about meaning what we say. Is there any promise we made, that we never did?" He may say, "You said you'd take us to church," or, "You said you'd play games with us," or whatever. Be willing to listen without criticism and make changes. Also ask, "Have I been inconsistent with following through on things I tell you to do or not to do? Have I been inconsistent by treating you differently than your siblings?" You'd be surprised what a difference seeing things from their perspective makes.

7. Bottom line: Make sure you mean what you say! If you don't mean it, don't say it!

THOUGHT QUESTIONS for Chapter 8

1. How important do you think consistency is to children?

2. Are there times other than correction in which it is important to be consistent?

3. What happens in a family when the parents have a "favorite" child?

CHAPTER 8:
MAINTAINING A CONSISTENT VIGIL

"Never give in--never, never, never, never; in nothing, great or small, large or petty— never give in except to convictions of honour and good sense. Never yield to force; never yield to the apparently overwhelming might of the enemy."

-Sir Winston Churchill[23]

"And thou shalt teach them diligently unto thy children, and shalt talk of them when thou sittest in thine house, and when thou walkest by the way, and when thou liest down, and when thou risest up." Deuteronomy 6:7

When builders in India illegally constructed a six-story structure in Rajasthan in 2010[24], they made many errors, not the least of which was using inferior materials. Inspectors had been called in to look at cracks in the building, and within minutes after their emerging from the structure, the entire building collapsed in a shower of cement, dust, and rebar! The footage of the sudden destruction was incredible! Amazingly, and thankfully, no one got hurt.

In the parenting process, it is easy for everything to look just right on the outside, but on the inside be built with inferior or unreliable materials. When the barricade is erected to keep the Devil out, it is imperative to use high-quality materials in the workmanship.

The job of the night watchman was one of the most important in the whole camp. It was his duty to keep the fire in the enclosure going, clang the tin cans to frighten away any beasts, and continuously scan the area for any sign of danger.

It may have been a boring job, and a lonely one, but it was extremely necessary. Each watchman understood the importance of his occupation, and took it very seriously. Any lapse in diligence could spell death for someone in the camp, even for him, so it was imperative that he continually and consistently did his job.

To take a break, or a night off, was unthinkable.

A chain is only as strong as its weakest link, a building is only as strong as its weakest block, and a barricade is only as strong as its least enforced part. Your weakest point is the one spot where the attacks will come, and it is that one spot which can cause the breakdown of the entire structure. Even excellent materials, if thrown together in a haphazard manner, will fall apart.

The most integral material we must use to build our barricade is the glue of consistency. Without it, we are playing with a strong possibility of the collapse of the family structure, and death of the residents of our home.

To my respondents, consistency was a huge factor in the formation of their lives. Jamie pointed out, "When my parents made up their mind about something, they didn't change, except on a very rare occasion—and then they always explained the change to us. Nothing was ever done on a haphazard basis. Their decisions were law."

Let's take a look at the three different ways these successful godly parents displayed consistency to their children.

"My Parents Were Faithful Through the Hard Times."

First of all, the parents displayed a **consistency in trials** that was a prime example of faith to the children.

With energy to spare, Brandon is a youth pastor and a plumber with a ready smile and quick wit. It didn't take a long conversation with him to realize that he had a good deal of maverick inside of him. But the example of his parents weighed heavy on his mind when it came time for him to make his own decision as to whether or not to attend church. "When I got older," he said, "I often thought of my parents, and how consistent they were through trials and tribulations. They stayed true to what they taught, and I realized that if they could do it all these years, that's what I wanted—even needed—to do."

During his growing-up years, Brandon had been a little spectator, watching his parents as they went through the struggles of life. He watched as they prayed, and learned as they trusted God through difficult circumstances. He rejoiced when the Lord showed Himself strong on their behalf, and also learned when God provided peace to endure. Through his parents' testimony of God's grace, Brandon knew deep down that he wanted to trust God too.

To see one of those young ones learn to depend on Him is worth every trial we have to endure.

Be willing to trust God and love Him through the hard times.

"My Parents Were Consistent in Discipline"

Many of their parents also were very **reliable in correction**. If an act was wrong once, it was wrong every time. In Steve's childhood it made a big difference. "My parents were definitely not lax," he said. "They were very consistent. Whatever they said, that was the way it was. I don't think they were harsh, because there was a lot of love, but rules were very consistent (dress, attitude, motives) yet implemented with love. They were enforced consistently, too, all the way through my youth, till I was out of the house."

This consistency creates in the child a deep respect for the boundaries. In the heart of a young person who's been taught consistently, "I don't want you to do this" really means something. There's no question of "maybe they don't really mean it this time"—it's an "I don't think I'd better do that EVER" attitude.

Children need boundaries. They need to know that there *are* limits to their behavior (by the way, there are limits to ours, too!), and that there are clear and consistent difficulties that occur when those limits are crossed. A study done by the Cooperative Extension of the North Carolina State University concluded:

> Research shows that children do better in life when they live with clear, consistent and fair rules. Parents often struggle with this

aspect of parenting, worrying that they are too strict or too lax, but saying "no" at times is actually a way of helping your children learn how they can survive in the world.[25]

Not only is it important to establish boundaries, but to consistently enforce them is equally important. Boundaries must be clear, and consistently enforced—or, in essence, there is no boundary at all. In fact, enforcement is so important that it is better to have a few rules and consistently apply them, than to have a hundred rules with haphazard enforcement.

Let your rules be few, and consistently enforced.

"My Parents Were Dependable in Spiritual Things"

In addition to consistency in discipline and in trials, several people commented on their parents' **consistency in devotion to God**. Robbie said, "My dad preached about how important it is for a Christian to read his Bible and pray at the same time, same place every day. One week, I got up at 4:45 every morning to see if Dad was really reading *his* Bible like he said a Christian should, and sure enough, he was there—every single morning."

What you do speaks so much louder than what you say! Even the secular world understands this when it comes to moral behavior. It comes as no surprise that a recent study by Caron Treatment Centers shows that parental influence in their manner of living has a much greater impact on young people than the actual words they as parents say. Parents may tell their children not to drink alcohol, but if they themselves imbibe, the message sent to the young people is clear: "It's OK to drink."

> Nearly a third of the 12 -18 year olds surveyed said they have observed one or both of their parents drinking alcohol to "relax" or "relieve stress" after a hard day (thirty-two percent). [26]

> Remember that even subtle behavior—such as having a drink after work in front of your child—can give a message about how you cope with stress.[27]

Many, many young people have been influenced to drink through the example of their own parents!

The positive side of this principle is also true: we can influence our children to right behavior through our example.

Positive parenting can be proven to transcend generations. In a September 2009 article, US News and World Report cites a study that was conducted on three generations of families in Oregon. The interesting article states:

> "Positive parenting"—including factors such as warmth, monitoring children's activities, involvement, and consistency of discipline—not only has positive impacts on adolescents, but on the way they parent their own children.

The project director, Deborah Capaldi, said,

> "This study is especially exciting because we had already identified processes by which risk behaviors and poor parenting may be carried across generations. Professor Kerr has now demonstrated that there is an additional pathway of intergenerational influence via positive parenting and development."[28]

This principle is beautifully portrayed in the Scriptures, telling us that, as we live our lives God's way, it leaves a lasting impression on the generations that follow us.

> And they that shall be of thee shall build the old waste places: thou shalt raise up the foundations of many generations; and thou shalt be called, The repairer of the breach, The restorer of paths to dwell in. (Isaiah 58:12)

Oh, that we could always remember how important it is to be spiritually consistent!

Be willing to love God enough to put Him and His righteousness first place.

Consistency in discipline, consistency through trials, and dependability in spiritual things are all positive things my respondents spoke about. But I would be only telling half the story if I stopped right there.

Right after mentioning how their parents' consistency was integral in their lives, my interviewees spoke of the many people they grew up with that did NOT have that advantage. In these cases, the outcome was disastrous. These Survivors told how their friends' parents were either inconsistent with all their children, or even sometimes with the youngest or favorite child.

****

"Lack of Consistency Undermined My Friends' Lives"

In my interviews, often a lack of consistency is cited as a reason for my respondents' friends not serving the Lord. "I know that the number one reason why my friends are not serving the Lord today is because of a lack of consistency in their parents' lives," Robbie explained. "My dad lived what he preached, was consistent in discipline, and therefore I never questioned God as a child. My friends did. For them, there was always the question, 'Does God really mean it?' in the back of their minds."

Angela agreed. "I believe the home life is very important," she said. "Many times parents are not consistent. They say and do one thing at church, but something different at home. Children get confused. A lot of folks are not really serious about living for God. In my observations, first-generation Christians need to get in all the way or they lose their kids. Many times that means the first-generation Christian will have to break ties with everything from their past life, but that it what it takes to raise a godly family."

Many Parents Relax As Their Children Become Teens

Consistency involves applying all the rules equally to all the children as long as the children are in the home. Unfortunately, this consistency doesn't happen often; some of my respondents told me that many parents allowed the rules to change as the children aged.

Brittany told me the story of a dear friend of hers: "I had one friend that I was especially close to. Consistency, or lack of it, was an issue. My friend's mother ran the home, and her father was weak. So when the kids got older and didn't want standards, the parents let them slip. Finally they got out of church altogether. Every once in a while I hear from my friend, and she's having some pretty tough marital problems. I know that lack of consistency is at the root of it."

It was a lesson she will never forget, and now Brittany's own child training philosophy embraces consistency thoroughly. "Be consistent, set rules and follow through," she stated. "There is a lot of security in consistency. There's got to be consistency, no matter what."

Be willing to love God and live consistently, even as the kids grow older—because to allow something to slip would be catastrophic.

It was a hot African night. Many of the men, thinking the lions were gone for good, had decided to sleep outside their tents. Even the night watchman was relaxed . . . too relaxed. As the lion suddenly crashed through the boma, the night watchman rubbed his eyes, stared in surprise, then screamed, "Simba! Simba!" Within seconds, everyone in the area was up and scrambling, some trying to get away, others throwing anything they could find at the animal—sticks, stones, and firebrands. But it was too late—the lion was already inside the barricade and going after his prey.

He broke through the horrified crowd of coolies and began dragging away one of poor fellows, in spite of all the yelling, screaming and racket going on around him. Having carried his prey just outside the fence, the lion was about to begin his meal when the second lion arrived. Together they devoured the man not thirty yards from the tent. Several people shot at the beasts, but they continued to munch as though nothing could deter them. It was a sickening sight to watch those huge animals consume that coolie so close to his tent-mates, and soon nothing remained but a few fragments.

The watchman's failure became another man's demise.

Parents Often Relax with their Youngest Child or the Favorite Child

I've seen it happen many, many times, and sometimes even to the best of families. Some parents start out with firm, consistent rules for their oldest children, but then allow the rules to change with the younger ones. Perhaps the parents are getting older and more tired, or maybe they feel as though they've "arrived already," or perhaps they've had their minds distorted through the philosophies of the world ("I learned better; I was very foolish when my older kids were young."). Several of the folks I interviewed remember this being the case with their youngest sibling.

Jamie, the older of two girls, notes that her younger sister seemed to get away with more as a teenager. Now her sister is a divorced mother of four, and lives a thoroughly immoral life. She told me, "My parents seem to overlook what she does, but I'm so afraid she will ruin their ministry. You name it, she's done it. She posts awful things on Facebook, and tells others that she dislikes the way she was raised. She seems to have no respect for Mom and Dad, but they just keep catering to her. I don't understand it."

"I've noticed over the years that the younger child is the most nonchalant with spiritual things. At least, that's the way it seems to me," she added.

Rachel shared a similar story of her youngest sister: "She is so very defiant to Mom and Dad, and she lives in her own place, but they still support her. I feel that my parents have somewhat shielded her from the realities of life. I wonder if maybe they are hindering her from hitting rock bottom, and I know that's where the Lord can really work in someone's life--when they're at the end of their rope. I don't really understand, but my parents don't like it when I try to tell them that they may be contributing to her rebellion."

We must be willing to deal consistently with all of our children, even if we get older and tired.

Many Parents Cater to Their "Favorite" Child.

Sometimes parent have a "favorite child" who is allowed more liberties than the other children, resulting in moral and spiritual catastrophe.

This situation was relayed to me on more than one occasion. Nick is a highly successful office manager, but also the product of a blended family. "My younger sister is actually my step-sister," he explained, "so there have been issues arising from the blended family. My parents were not consistent with her. Maybe they felt bad for her or something, but they let her have some liberties the others didn't have. It seemed to have a bad effect on her. It didn't help that she spent her summers with her biological dad where she could do whatever she wanted. Her childhood had very little consistency. Of course, she's not in church now." Perhaps there was very little Nick's parents could do about the rules at his sister's biological dad's place, but consistency at their own home would have made a big difference. (See Elizabeth's story in the chapter "The Exceptions.")

One of the saddest interviews I ever had was with Larry, who was raised in a Christian home and has several adult children himself now. Much of his gray hair comes from worrying about his daughter, who chose to live a loose life and is now in an abusive home. His words of wisdom come from many sleepless nights of praying, thinking, and soul-searching.

"Inconsistencies in the parents kill spiritual desire in young people," Larry said. "I've seen it many times. There are several ways parents can be inconsistent. Sometimes parents behave one way in church and another way at home, and sometimes they laugh at a child's behavior one time, then spank him for the very same behavior later. But one of the most serious forms of inconsistency is when one parent wants the affection of a child and will undermine the other parent in order to win the child's affection. We've seen it happen in our own home, and it was disastrous. Now that she's older, our daughter simply dislikes both my wife and I, and is in an abusive relationship. It's terribly heartbreaking."

In essence, Larry was saying that those who try to win the affection of a "favorite" child do so because they themselves feel the need to be loved.

Perhaps the parents did not get the approval from their own mother and father that they so desperately needed, and they transfer that need for approval to their own children. Many people seek security from another human being, and it's simply not going to happen. No person on earth can give us the love and approval that we crave from God alone. The problem is that most people misunderstand that gnawing in their heart, and feel that their need can be met by another person—but only God can meet those deep inner needs. He alone is our sufficiency; He is our all-in-all.

Be willing to love God and seek **Him** *for our approval, so that we can meet our children's needs for consistency.*

Not long ago, my family and I were at a church in the northeast. It was a Missions Conference, and I was pleasantly surprised to hear a report from a single lady missionary who had been raised in a godly Christian home. Her very interesting story began when she was just a little girl. "I was raised in a hunter's home," Emily told us. I could sense the interest of the men in the congregation. "My dad was a big hunter, and there were lots of weapons in our house. He took the time to teach each of us the importance of respecting the weapons, so that by the time we were four years old, we were allowed to have our own bow and arrow . . . as long as we didn't shoot each other!" Laughter gently rippled through the crowd.

"One day when I was four, I got angry with my sister, and I shot an arrow at her!" She paused for a few seconds, and then continued, chuckling, "So what happens when you get in trouble in a Christian home? I got a spanking!" Several folks laughed and nodded their heads in understanding.

"So, as I was lying on my bed, crying, suddenly everything my parents and

Sunday school teacher had been trying to tell me all came together, and I realized *I* was a sinner. There on my bed, I stopped crying and prayed and asked the Lord to forgive me of my sins. Even though I was so young, it was the best day of my life."

Emily smiled and continued, "So, parents and grandparents . . . you keep doing what you know is right! Do it consistently! You never know – someday it may lead to your children's salvation!"

May we learn from these dear people, and be consistent!

LIONPROOF STRATEGY #7:
BE CONSISTENT!

PREPARING YOUR DEFENSE:

1. If you have several children, take the time to do some heart-searching. Do you baby your youngest? Do you have a favorite? Is there one child that may get more privileges than others for no good reason?

2. Are there exceptions to your rules? Decide how often you will allow exceptions. (Keep in mind that human nature likes to turn the exception into the *new* rule!)

ASSIGNMENT:

Take some time with your spouse and discuss your rules of your home. Write down as many of them as you can think of. How will you enforce the rules? Do your children know them? Are they few in number? Make your list as complete as you can without taking too long for this activity. Too many rules can be worse than none at all.

Date completed_____

Finally, be prepared to enforce your rules. **Remember, a rule which is not enforced is no rule at all.**

THOUGHT QUESTIONS for Chapter 9:

1. What do you think is the key to passing on your values?

2. Is it possible to have a good relationship with your children?

3. Is it possible to have a good relationship with <u>each</u> of your children?

4. What do you think can be accomplished when you have your child's heart?

CHAPTER 9:
YOUR MOST VALUABLE WEAPON

You will always be your child's favorite toy.~Vicki Lansky[29]

My son, give me thine heart, and let thine eyes observe my ways.(Proverbs 23:26)

The other day I was talking with Lacy, ashy middle-aged mom, and we came upon the subject of her childhood. She spoke freely, knowing her words would be helpful to others. What she said sent chills up my spine: "We could talk to Mom about anything. She was always open, honest, and available. But if I tried to talk to Dad about anything, he always cut me off and said I should not talk like that. I guess I might have tried maybe four or five times, but when you get cut off like that, after a while you give up. At least, that's what I did. I just never talked to my dad about anything after that."

As she spoke, my mind was buzzing. At least her mother is a very strong person, and willing to do whatever it takes to keep her children's hearts. I know her well, but her father is very quiet and didn't seem to like to be bothered by his children.

Lacy's story was not ideal, but she turned out to love and serve the Lord anyway. She knew she could confide in her mother, and knowing her mom, I feel she received excellent guidance as she was growing up. But I wonder how much better could it have been if she could talk freely to both of her parents?

One of the most potent weapons we have at our disposal as parents is having our child's heart. "I think it's very important for the parent to have the child's heart, especially the mother," Jennifer explained. "The child knows he can go to Mom about anything, and she will listen to him. And if he's willing to listen to her advice, she can then help the child deal with situations correctly. This kind of 'give and take' can go a long way in helping the young person."

When our children are young, they naturally desire to cling to us parents—especially to their mother. It seems like we can hardly turn around, but that they are virtually under our feet! But, as time goes by, if we do nothing to keep their hearts, they begin looking to others who will listen to them and understand them.

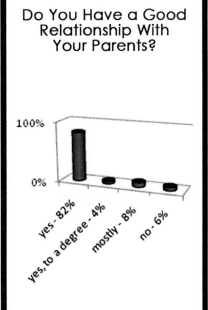

Looking to others, particularly to peers, can be a dangerous thing. Remember what happened to Rehoboam in 1 Kings, when he took the advice of his peers, rather than the counsel of his father's older, wise advisors? He lost just about everything he had; his "loyal" subjects were not so loyal anymore! The same thing may just happen to a young person who rejects the advice of his elders, and embraces the hot-headed ways of the younger generation.

For his future's sake, it's very important that we have our child's heart. A good relationship is our most valuable weapon.

How do successful parents keep their children's hearts? There are three factors: Making Home Happy, Pulling Family Together, and learning to Be Approachable.

Making Home Happy

"A merry heart doeth good like a medicine" Proverbs 17:22

Megan is a tall, elegant southern belle with a warm personality and engaging smile. Her childhood was full of happy memories. "In my home," she said, "there were a lot of No's, but a lot of Yes's too.

"Mom and Dad had a good balance, it seems to me. Daddy did everything with us, sometimes even staying up 'till two AM playing Monopoly, even though he hated Monopoly. He would do whatever we wanted to do, go wherever we wanted to go, and stay as long as we wanted to stay. We never felt deprived. We had lots of toys; we even had a pool, a trampoline, four-wheelers—all sorts of things to do. Daddy was very strict, but we were so busy having fun with all the things we *could* do, we didn't focus on the stuff we *couldn't* do.

"We never went to our friends' house," she continued. "They always came to ours, because ours was so much fun. I know now that Daddy did that on purpose, so he could keep an eye on us to make sure we were doing right and being protected. And our friends were glad to come over; to them, our house was *the* place to be!"

Like Megan, 98% of the people I talked to responded positively when I asked them if their childhood was happy. Many of them echoed a very similar story to Megan's. The parents worked hard to make home a happy place. Even serving the Lord was something the parents tried to make joyful, as Shari attests:

"One thing I noticed," she said, "—and when I became an adult my mom told me she purposely did this --was that my parents never complained about the ministry to us kids! Also, any time we "had" to be at church extra for services (set up and clean up) my dad would make sure to emphasize that we were "getting" to serve, not "having" to! He would also reward us in other ways for helping out when we were there. He made it a joy to serve the Lord!"

As a side note, every one of Shari's five brothers and sisters are serving the Lord—by their own choice, as adults with their own families. What an amazing legacy!

Unfortunately, the tendency is to neglect our family as we get busier—especially as we become more involved in ministry.It can be very easy to look after someone else's family while virtually ignoring our own. We would like to think that pastors have better success with their families, but we actually find that the reverse is often true.

While on church visitation one day, I came upon a dilapidated mobile home. The grass desperately needed mowing, toys were strewn about aimlessly, and the cobwebs around the doorframe were thick and well-populated. A young lady came to the door, and we engaged in some light conversation. I noticed the tattoos on her arm, and her abundance of piercings. When asked whether she attended church anywhere, she waved her hand nonchalantly. "Oh, I don't bother with that. My dad is a pastor," she replied, as though that explained it. Though I didn't have much success in getting her to think about coming to church, I know I went away wondering what had happened in her life to push her away from God.

How are pastor's families often affected by the ministry?

- **Eighty percent** believe pastoral ministry has **negatively** affected their families. Many pastor's children do not attend church now because of what the church has done to their parents.

- **Eighty percent** of adult children of pastors surveyed have had to seek **professional help for depression.**[30]

I think that, as far as pastors are concerned, busyness is the main issue.

- **Ninety** percent of the pastors report working between **55** to **75** hours per week.

- **Eighty** percent of spouses feel the pastor is overworked.[31]

There's no doubt that the ministry is a difficult place to raise children, and many young people may be tempted to think, "Well, if my parents weren't in the ministry, I would have things easier." However, Steve, whom we met earlier, said that his dad's advice on this subject helped him through many rough spots as a young person. "My dad often said, 'Son, it's tough anywhere —get used to it!' He pulled me close, and showed me the reality of life. Even now that I am a pastor many of the things he did and said come to mind."

But it's not only those in the ministry who are busy. Gone are the days of the slow-paced rural lifestyle the average American enjoyed in the past two hundred years. It has been replaced by the frantic pace that all of our conveniences afford! We invent techno-gadgets to help us save time, and we feverishly run from activity to activity in a whirlwind of social networking, ball games, texting, clubs, and internet-surfing.

According to a recent UK study, the average working parent spends only nineteen minutes a day with his or her children.[32] Then, where multiple children are involved, it is more difficult to spend time with each child individually. Undoubtedly, it is an uphill battle to have an influence on our children.

The parents of the folks I've interviewed were obviously very busy people. Not only did they work their jobs, but they also attended church at least three times a week, went on weekly visitation, and attended revival meetings. Also, many were involved in various ministries: driving the church bus, teaching Sunday school, or leading a Bible study. These extremely busy people still were willing to lay aside their own "me time," of which they had precious little, to listen to their young person.

Along with being a fifth-generation Christian, Brittany is a busy mother of three active boys herself. "Many parents are just too busy to spend time with their children," she told me. "When something needs dealt with, they think, 'I'll deal with it later,' 'but' later' never comes. Often those that don't work a job but are still somehow too 'busy' for their children are just selfish – not caring."

Arianna put it this way: "It's important that the parents spend time with the kids and really pay attention to them—in addition to taking them to church. If they only pay attention to them when they are doing wrong, they [the children] will be trained to do wrong to get attention!

"When a parent feels like they have to work more to gain more money, they are actually putting the emphasis on material things. Kids don't need more *things* – they need their parents' *time.*"

As parents, we must do what we can to connect with our own children. We may not be able to do as many fun and exciting things as some can, but we can do our best to make the time necessary to bond with our kids. Many of these first-generation parents felt it necessary to say "no" to all sorts of tempting activities in order to spend time with their families. If we follow the example of those godly parents, we will reap many benefits!

Pull together as a family

A very closely related principle of successful parents is the fact that they do their best to pull their family together. In the world of nature, a lion goes for the lone straggler; he rarely attacks a whole group of people. There is great strength in numbers. And not just a group of people, but a group of people *together* – stability through *unity*!

I would not be able to put in this book the vast number of testimonies given that tell how the families did things together. Some young people were homeschooled; and though that alone does not guarantee success, it does help to eliminate one of the avenues that Satan uses to destroy families: divide and conquer! The latter part of the twentieth century showed how young people could be driven into the world by cutting them off from their parents. Now, as we are in the twenty-first century, families continue to fragment through the vast array of individualistic opportunities that have come through technology.

In 2009, Psychology Today described the changing family:

> Many of us remember when dinnertime regularly brought the nuclear family together at the end of the day—everyone having finished work, homework, play, and sports. Parents and children relaxed, shared their day's experiences, kept up with each other's lives, and actually made eye contact while they talked.
>
> Now, dinnertime tends to be a much more harried affair. With e-mailing, video chatting, and TVs blaring, there is little time set aside for family discussion and reflection on the day's events. Conversations at meals sometimes resemble instant messages where family members pop in with comments that have no linear theme. In fact, if there is time to have a family dinner, many family members tend to eat quickly and run back to their own computer, video game, cell phone or other digital activity.[33]

One day I talked to Doug, a first-generation Christian who is the father of several adult Survivors. As we spoke, his normally bright face became serious. "My dad worked second shift," he told me. "So whenever we came home from school he was at work. Of course, he didn't get home until long after I was in bed. I don't even remember seeing him in the morning before I went to school.

"But on weekends, I have vivid memories of my dad, sitting in front of the television watching sports. It didn't matter what sport was on—baseball, football, or whatever, he sat and watched it. Then, when the game was over, he got up and went out to mow the lawn, or to do some other work. It was a rare thing that we did something together as a family. I tried to change that with my children; I wanted to be there for them."

David, whom we met earlier, also feels it's important for families to be together. "Families just don't seem to have much time together to bond," he explained. "If someone were to ask my advice on how to raise godly children, I would tell them to enjoy their children! We never felt our children were a burden. They were always a joy and a blessing. We never wanted to just 'get away' from our kids. We did lots of things together, but especially we played family games, and we read a *lot* of books together out loud."

The Survivors know that one of the most influential activities in their lives was the fact that their families did things together. Though their parents had opportunities to pursue their own individual activities (like watch TV, play computer games, or talk on the phone), they instead invested their time in their children, reaping a tremendous return.

Joanne shared how her parents pulled together as a family. She told me, "Dad never had hobbies, nor did Mom. The family always did things as a unit. Anything they wanted to do, we loaded up as a family and did it. One of the things we did together every year was going to camp meeting. It was a really good thing for us. Also, we always sang together since I was 6 or 7. We were a very tight-knit family, probably because we homeschooled. In fact, we're still very close, even now that my brother and I have families of our own."

One young man told me that his family worked together to clean the church, while another said they sang together. Still another, Brandon, said that his dad took him out on visitation with him. "Looking back," Brandon said, "I realized that one of the most important things my parents did that helped me to serve God was the fact that they always involved us in ministry. My dad was just starting the church, and he needed all the help he could get, so we were called upon to do a lot. We did a lot of ministry together during that time. I didn't realize it at the time, but it was one of the most formative things they could have done."

Nightfall brought a familiar pang to the lion, and he made his way through the dense jungle to a camp where he knew the Indian men were sleeping. It would be an easy meal; the humans' lack of horns and hooves made them go down effortlessly. He quickened his pace, roaring as he went.

All too soon he found his desired spot, and crept in slowly for the attack. All was silent, except for the occasional clanging of tin cans, which the large cat had become accustomed to. In fact, it almost sounded like a dinner bell. With a flick of his tail, he stole closer.

Fourteen coolies lay peacefully sleeping in the tent when he sprang. He broke through the tent, landing on two of the men. Amidst yelps of terror, he quickly grabbed his prey and bounded away. This time, however, he dropped it in disgust not far from the tent.

It was a bag of rice.

The wild-eyed coolies realized their close call, and could not contain their emotions. Shaking with utter horror, they gesticulated wildly and loudly chattered. Theirs was a close call, and their thankfulness knew no bounds.

Striving together toward a common goal has a way of pulling people together. You could take the most irritable hound dogs and put them together on a hunt, and they will quit fighting each other in order to get the job done. Sometimes we may feel like those quarrelling hound dogs, always at each others' throats. But if we pull together to get something done, we will find that the Lord will help us develop a unity we haven't known before.

Memories made of playing or working together can be very precious. Even hard times endured together have a way of bonding a family together. One of my grown children told me recently, "Some of my most wonderful memories were the difficulties we went through while we traveled – a flat tire, a mechanical problem, or something that broke. It was always exciting to see how God was going to help us through that situation." For us, these memories create a powerful pull that draws the hearts of older children closer to their parents.

So, make some memories. Pull the family together and do something: clean the church, sing at a nursing home, or work the bus ministry. Do something together, whatever it is. And don't fret over the hard times, because God can use them to bind you together. Doing activities together may be just the thing to create a protective barrier from the blood-thirsty attacks of Satan.

Be Approachable

Another important quality of successful parents is that they are welcoming and easy to talk to.

> During a particularly interesting interview, Shaunna and her husband, both second generation Christians, took turns cuddling their newborn baby as they answered my questions. "When we were growing up," Shaunna said, "we often had questions, and Dad didn't seem to think that questioning was rebellion. He understood the spirit of questioning things; we just wanted to know how or why. And he was honest if he didn't know the answer. His openness really helped me as I was growing up."

In fact, 58% of our respondents agreed with Shaunna. Many of them said, "They were always available to talk to me whenever I needed them!"

Robbie's wife Angela explained it this way: "I was very close to both of my parents. I had a very good relationship with them, and I still do to this day. They were very approachable as we were growing up, and they still are. My sisters and I talk about that sometimes, and I think it played a key role in our lives. Now, one of my sisters is an associate pastor's wife, another plays piano for a church and teaches at a Christian college, and another sister is a teacher at a Christian school. I'd say my parents did an excellent job."

Herein is one of the keys: "they would be available to talk whenever I needed them." They were not able to talk only on certain scheduled times, but *at the time when they were needed*. Many people are under the erroneous assumption that when their children become teenagers, they no longer need their parents as much as they used to. But young people need to be able to communicate with their parents, and we as parents need to be available to listen to them when they are willing to talk.

The nature photographer spends hours waiting for the proper shot. His subject—perhaps an elusive white-tailed buck—is completely unpredictable, and is as likely to run as it is to display that coveted twelve-point rack of his. The photographer must get into position and patiently wait for just the right opportunity. It may take hours, but to get a good shot, that's what he needs to do.

> So when the unexpected happens—and with animals, it often does
> —I sometimes have to take a little more time on the job. But when
> I see the end result—those cute pictures of raccoons or squirrels on
> a calendar or postcard—it makes the waiting worthwhile.[34]
> —Nature Photographer, BJU Press, Math 3, pg. 49

Aren't our children more valuable than a photograph? Isn't it worthwhile to be there when they are ready to talk? I would say so.

But, young people can be completely unpredictable. We never know just when they will open up and begin to talk, and we must be ready when that time comes. It is the difference between a simple "deer picture" and a beautiful wildlife portrait!

"Mom would listen, no matter how long it took," Brittany told me. "My mom always knew when something was wrong. Sometimes she came into my room, and as soon as she stepped in the door, Mom would ask, 'What's wrong?'

"'Nothing,' was my reply. Of course, Mom didn't believe me. She sat down with me and just piece by piece drew it out. In fact, she wouldn't leave until I talked! Sometimes it seemed to take forever for me to open up, but I always felt better after talking to Mom."

In true communication, there is a lot of talking *and* listening. We parents tend to monopolize conversations, but there is a lot more benefit if the young people open up. In addition, I've discovered that if I'm willing to take the time to listen to them, they are more likely to listen to me. *Then* there is true communication.

Good communication is the bedrock of a good relationship, and a good relationship is vital to the transfer of values. When good communication begets a good relationship, parents are able to be very candid. "When I was eighteen," Steve explained, "I remember backsliding for a bit. I remember my mom telling me, 'Steve, you know I didn't raise you to serve the Devil. I would rather you die than serve the Devil.' Because I was close to her, her words really had an impact on my life. She was able to say some extremely hard things to me, because I knew how much she loved me. I just needed my cage rattled to bring me back to reality."

It didn't seem to matter in the interviews whether the young person was closer to Mom or to Dad growing up. What mattered most was that they had a good relationship with their parents, and felt that they could talk to their parents. In fact, 82% said they had a good relationship with their parents.

Neil, whom we met earlier, said, "A very famous evangelist was preaching revival meetings at our church, and there were also some notable musicians. The ladies sang a song about one of the girls' family who died in a fire. The only thing I could think of for the rest of the night was, "If I was in the fire, I would be in hell." That night I couldn't sleep, so I began pacing the floor. Eventually, my dad saw me, and asked me what was wrong. It was real late— maybe midnight or later—but Dad took the time to lead me to Christ. I'm so thankful he was willing to help me even though it was the middle of the night."

This dear young man found his parents to be a source of comfort and strength to him as he was growing up. Because of that, he was able to get the help he needed to make an important decision that had an eternal impact!

I must also mention the importance of young people making spiritual decisions. We tend to think narrowly: *I'm so glad he got saved! Now hopefully he will make wise choices.* But if we truly thought through the ramifications of his salvation, we would realize how great of an impact such a decision will have— not just on him, but on an untold number of people. When one of our children decides to turn to righteousness, turns to God from his own way, there is a tremendous eternal impact:

- His life becomes radically changed for the better; he becomes a more obedient, loving, and selfless child. This in itself can have a life-altering impact on the rest of the family.

- His own eternity is secure and settled, for he has gone from being a child of the devil to a child of God. All of eternity for him has been changed. He is now a recipient of the entire wealth of God Himself. (being heirs of God through Christ)

- His life becomes one of seeking to please God, rather than seeking to please himself. As such, he will have an impact on the other young people around him, pointing them to the Savior to whom he himself has turned. Because of his experience of being born-again, he will seek to lead others to the Lord.

- When one of our children leads someone to the Lord, then THEIR eternity has been altered from death to life!

Awhile back I got a text from my daughter which said, "I got to lead a young lady to the Lord today! I AM SO EXCITED!!" She was thrilled; I was ecstatic! It is a joy like no other. It is also sobering to realize that if *she* hadn't gotten saved years ago, then this other person probably would not have gotten saved either.

Do you see how this can snowball? Through the salvation of one, many more can be reached. Just as one kernel of corn can grow into a corn stalk that yields perhaps three or four ears of corn with roughly eight hundred kernels on each ear (about 2,400 to 3,200 kernels per stalk!), so the salvation of one young person can yield a multitude in Heaven! Conversely, a decision to put off salvation, or to refuse to live for God, could doom many, many people to an eternity in the lake of fire. The salvation of our children is something we cannot take lightly!

Our children's salvation does not entirely depend on us as parents. However, it is possible that *the amount of time they spend in interaction with a parent helps develop their maturity,* and a mature person can more easily understand the eternal ramifications of their decisions. Guiding our children as they think through life's ponderous subjects is not only a good idea, it is absolutely necessary!

One of the main reasons why I think being available to our children is highly important is because of:

A Surprising Discovery

An astonishing result of my study has been the number of respondents who were actually firstborn children. As a matter of fact, I didn't realize it might be a factor until I was toward the end of my interviews. I was actually lying in bed one night pondering about the folks I've interviewed, when I realized that the vast majority of them were firstborns. (Later I would discover that sixty-eight percent were firstborn children. The next highest group, second-borns, was WAY behind at fourteen percent.) My mind began racing as I considered the implications this finding could have. As you might suspect, I didn't get much sleep that night!

It is possible that birth order may have a tremendous impact on whether or not young people will dedicate their lives to serving the Lord. By birth order, I mean whether or not your child is the firstborn son or daughter, or whether they are a second son, or a second daughter, etc. Because of family dynamics, both an oldest son and oldest daughter are considered firstborns. Also, when there is a space of about five years between children, the younger child is almost like another firstborn. Hence, it is possible to have several firstborns in the same family. For more detailed information and additional study about this topic, read the fascinating book, <u>The New Birth Order Book</u>, by Kevin Leman. Though I don't agree with everything that is written, it is still very helpful in understanding both ourselves and our children.

I realize that this is something completely different that has never been discussed in many Bible-believing circles, and as such, may cause a great rise of irritation. However, I beg you to briefly consider a few thoughts:

Though birth order may have a correlation with whether or not our children serve the Lord, I believe that it is not only the birth order itself which can heighten a child's spiritual perceptivity, but also increased interaction alone with a parent. Harold McCurdy quoted British scientist Sir Francis Galton in his work titled *The Childhood Pattern of Genius*:

> The elder sons have, on the whole, decided advantages of nurture over the younger sons. They are more likely to become possessed of independent means, and therefore are able to follow the pursuits that are the most attractive to their taste; they are treated more as companions by their parents, and have earlier responsibility, both of which would develop independence of character; probably, also, the first-born child of families not well-to-do in the world would generally have more attention in his infancy, more breathing space, and better nourishment than his younger brothers and sisters in their several turns.[35]

The reason why I believe birth order is important is because of the results of McCurdy's research project.

In addition, it is a well-established (and researched) fact throughout history that removing a child from his peers and placing him with loving, affectionate adults, while giving him the freedom to pursue his own curiosities, is a recipe for genius.[36]

Consider some of the most influential inventors of our time:

Thomas Edison, the inventor of electric lights, the phonograph, the motion picture and more, was thrown out of school by a teacher who thought he was "addled." "He will never learn!" she told his parents. But his mother spent hour after hour with him, carefully, consistently, and lovingly teaching him to read, write, and figure.

Moriah Mitchel, educated at home by her persistent and quick-witted Quaker father, became one of the first female astronomers, making discoveries and advancements in the field of astronomy that became a boon to society.

George Washington Carver, the great agricultural chemist and developer of peanut butter and a vast array of other peanut products, spent countless hours with his adoptive family and fell in love with nature as a young boy. Soon he became known as "The Plant Doctor," and eventually used his knowledge and ability to greatly benefit the southern states and the common worker after the Civil War.

These are just a few examples of the benefits of parental influence in the life of a young person. You may say, "That's all well and good for geniuses, but I don't see what that has to do with me and my family." At first glance it appears to be completely unrelated. It is true that we are not striving to create geniuses—we are seeking to have a *godly* generation. However, I believe the principles remain the same for a mental genius as it is for a spiritual giant: to develop maturity in a young person through consistent parental/adult influence. Then he will be equipped to make right decisions.

Now, here comes the important part: I believe maturity depends on two things:

- *the amount of time a young person spends with a parent*, and
- *learning to work hard.*

With maturity comes a spiritual vision—*an ability to see the impact of eternity*—and the ability to make wise decisions based on eternal facts.

I have seen many young people raised in godly homes who have learned to be responsible by working hard and spending a lot of time with a loving, caring adult. Almost without fail, these fine young people make wise decisions based on a spiritual vision of eternity, and they enter their adult lives, bringing glory to the Lord. Conversely, I have seen a vast multitude of young folks who entered their adult lives immature, and made unwise decisions based on lack of spiritual vision. Now they are spending the rest of their lives paying dearly for their mistakes.

I realize that it is God who draws the sinner to Himself, but could it be that He may also use the time and effort spent with a loving parent? Could that be the main reason why so many young people who are left on their own day after day seem to have no concept or desire for eternal things? I believe it is entirely possible.

The application to this principle is vastly important. First of all, please do not think that all is lost for your younger children. You cannot change the order your children come to you. It is what they call an "unchangeable." But, knowing the statistics, you can do your best to counterbalance that by increasing your influence on the younger children. Knowing your older child already has a built-in advantage, you may want to very carefully consider the amount of time you spend with your younger children individually.

Regardless of your application of this theory, parental influence cannot be overstated. In a day when parents are expected to "do their own thing" and leave the kids to do theirs as well, spending time with your children is definitely going against the current tide, but it is nonetheless necessary. I believe that if we are willing to "fall into the ground and die," (die to our own desires and pursuits), we will "bring forth much fruit," with our children making prudent decisions for the Lord and living for Him.

Sometimes life is not ideal

Of course, being available to talk with our children at any time of day or night is ideal, but sometimes life isn't perfect—or perhaps it's we who are not perfect! Some of the folks I talked to had a stiff relationship with their parents.

"My parents were approachable, but only to a degree," Tracy explained. "We didn't talk about a lot of things, and there was not a lot of verbal affirmation or physical affection. I really wasn't free to talk about questions about guys or growing up. Sometimes I could talk about friends, or about relationships, but not about normal struggles in my life. It was somewhat like going to the manager of a store. And I knew they loved me, but I also knew they were more open with my younger sister than with me.

"If they had been more approachable, I know it would have saved me from a lot of the heartaches that I went through."

In most situations, however, at least *one* of the parents was approachable. Though the ideal would be that a young person could talk freely to *both* parents, this was not always the case. From this, I would surmise that it is very important that at least *one* parent makes it his or her goal to be available to talk when the young person has the need.

****

Sitting in the empty sanctuary one evening, Abby and I were talking of her teenage years. She spoke fondly of her father's involvement in her life, her family's many ministries they did together, and her life as a teenager. I could see that her heart was open to me, and she was talking easily.

I asked her the question I always asked when we talked about this time period of someone's life. "So how were rules enforced while you were young, and especially as you got older?" She drew in her breath, looked thoughtfully at the wall, and replied, "I'm not sure what to tell you. I wasn't a perfect kid, by any stretch, but I never wanted to disappoint my father. I knew he would be terribly hurt if I went astray, and I just never wanted to disappoint him."

At first it was an answer that stunned me, but as I looked back at my own childhood I realized that it was *this* factor, in addition to the fear of God, that drove me to be who I am. *I* never wanted to disappoint my parents.

It's the deep-seated desire to please someone you love; to be someone of whom he or she can be proud. It is that desire to please which causes a young person to rise up and do something great, to go the distance, to accomplish a goal, and to reach a height previously thought unattainable. That same desire to please a godly parent carries with it purity, godly character and a love for God, as well as an aversion to sin.

After that interview, I started hearing the very same answer time and again from my respondents:

"When I was growing up and we did something against the rules," Rachel told me. "Sometimes privileges were taken away. More often than not, though, we just got a good talkin' to. Mom or Dad would say, 'I'm disappointed in you, for these reasons . . .' and then go on to tell me what I did wrong and why it broke their heart.

> "To me, those talks were worse than a whoopin'. It was a heart-wrenching sick-to-my stomach feeling when I found out I disappointed my parents. I guess when I hurt my mom or dad, it would hurt me.
>
> "I think I got to the age where I realized that they wanted the best for me, and they loved me more than life itself. It was just heartbreaking to think that I would hurt someone who loved me so much. For me, the effect was that *I would do almost anything rather than disappoint Mom and Dad.*"

Holding her three-month old baby on her lap, Joanne remarked, "I guess I would say that the strength of my relationship with my parents determined the course of my life. Because I knew they loved me, and I loved them, I rarely broke the rules as I got older. I just always wanted to please them."

Micah agreed. "At first, I just wanted to uphold my dad's name; he's a pastor of a big church, you know. Finally, I decided to serve God on my own. One time, I did something that hurt my dad, and it broke my heart. I had learned to fear my dad, and it became a fear for God. God became REAL to me."

Another young man, Josh is a man of few words. His perception is as precise as his sniper bullets in the Special Forces. "I remember getting to a point where I was too big to spank," he remarked. "That was about the time when I started to realize I didn't want to disappoint my father. I was around thirteen at the time, and I just still did what Mom and Dad wanted me to do, because I loved them and didn't want to hurt them."

Leaning forward, Josh continued, "My dad wasn't just a father...*he was a friend.*"

Thomas Edison, the great inventor, gave the credit for his success to his mother who deeply influenced him. "My mother was the making of me," Edison explained. "She was so true, so sure of me; and I felt I had something to live for, someone I must not disappoint."[37]

Edison's mother influenced him in temporal things; how much better is the eternal influence of a godly set of parents?

Herein is your primary offensive weapon: have your child's heart, and he or she will never want to disappoint you.

LIONPROOF STRATEGY #8:
HAVE Your CHILD'S HEART!

STRATEGY #9:
BE APPROACHABLE!

PREPARING YOUR DEFENSE:

1. What are some of the ways you think Satan is dividing families?

2. James 1:19 says, "Wherefore, my beloved brethren, let every man be swift to hear, slow to speak, slow to wrath . . . " How does this apply in the home?

3. Since relationships rise and fall on communication, list some steps you can take to increase communication with your children. (Note: I did not mean *lecture more* – I mean real, live, two-way communication!)

Assignment:

1. Take some time to evaluate your relationship to each of your children. Do any of your relationships need any bolstering? Take a piece of paper and write down your thoughts.

    Date Completed:_____

2. Spend time praying about each child, asking God to reveal to you how best to develop a strong relationship with them.

    Date Completed:_____

Thought Questions on Chapter 10:

1. How does the parents' attitude toward authority affect their kids?

2. In your opinion, how does parental anger affect children?

3. How does bitterness affect children?

CHAPTER 10:
BARRIERS TO OBTAINING THE MOST VALUABLE WEAPON:
WHY MOST PEOPLE DON'T HAVE THEIR CHILD'S HEART

"But if ye bite and devour one another, take heed that ye be not consumed one of another."
(Galatians 5:15)

Have you ever wondered if there was a missing element in most parenting philosophies? Have you ever seen families who seem to have everything just right, and yet they still lose their children to the world? Could there be something, some insidious practice or philosophy, that has crept in to these families to steal away their children?

Sometimes we put ourselves into a position where we make it easy for Satan to launch an attack. Anything that puts a barrier or a wedge between you and your child is a potential area for deception, division, and finally consumption by the prowling lion! If we're not careful, Satan will come upon us, invade our homes, and take our children unawares.

Few parenting books, if any, deal with the topic with which I am about to deal. Whether the writers think it unnecessary, or whether they simply do not realize its importance, I don't know. Though it is a dynamic which is almost wholly overlooked, it may make all the difference in a child's life. A parent can do everything right (speaking merely from outward appearance) and still fail miserably at this one point. But this one point is one of the most crucial elements, while at the same time one of the most overlooked, in parenting.

Criticizing Authority

Every one of the second-generation Christians I interviewed energetically agreed that **it is detrimental to a child's spiritual growth to criticize a spiritual leader in front of them.** Many of them told about friends whose parents complained about a Christian leader or someone else in the church. In **every case**, it was damaging to the young person. Dianne told me, "My older brother went away from the Lord. It started in junior high, probably as a result of a split in our church. Some of the deacons were saying bad things about the church, and it was nasty. To this day, my mother thinks that all the complaints and criticism caused the church to lose ground in my brother's mind. He felt that my dad had been treated unjustly, and maybe he was. Then to top it off, we went through difficult financial times because of the split, and I think my brother ended up with some bitterness through that whole ordeal. He doesn't serve the Lord at all today."

Another young lady, Angela, told me her experience. "I would say that of all the friends I had in church, the ones that didn't make it seem to be the ones whose parents got on "the outs" with the pastor."

Joanna also told me about one of her good friends. "His mom never backed up his dad," she said. "His dad always wanted to live for God, but he never had the support of his wife. She was always supplanting him and belittling him. I could see it, even though I was just a friend. It really affected my friend. To this day, it's obvious that God's not real to him. It's so sad."

> Do you think it is harmful for a parent to criticize an authority in front of the children?
>
> ## 88% said YES!

One of the most telling, and most credible words of wisdom comes from Brittany, a fifth-generation Christian. This dear family has had generation after generation serving the Lord, many of them full-time. "One of the keys to our family's success is the fact that my parents never said *anything* negative about the pastor, assistant pastor, or any staff member. My mom worked in the church office, so I'm sure she had plenty of opportunities to see inconsistencies or hear about problems, but never once did she bring any of them home to us. Through their example, we learned to respect authority."

Robbie spoke with clarity about the effect of criticizing authorities. "For one thing," he said, "I think a lot of the young people who leave good churches do so because they're simply not saved. I know it was that way with a lot of my peers. But I believe a big part of the problem is actually a parental problem: parents having inconsistencies. Instead of praying for the preacher, they would **prey on** the preacher! By talking about and criticizing the preacher at home, they actually feed rebellion in their kids' lives. The child then has no authority, and is left to himself. Of course, we know that 'a child left to himself bringeth his mother to shame.' Being critical of an authority almost **damns** the child. I've seen it over and over, not only as a young person myself, but also as a youth worker and assistant pastor.

These dear people tell us that complaining about our authorities is like pulling the rug out from under our children, giving them unstable footing for their lives.

Being critical of those in authority is highly damaging to a young person. As parents, we can be tempted to think, *I have every right to voice my opinion. I'm an American citizen, and freedom of speech is part of the Bill of Rights!* That is true, but we must be careful how and to whom we voice our opinions. If there is a problem with an authority, we must be certain to follow the instructions given to us from the Lord for any situation involving conflict with another believer:

> "Moreover if thy brother shall trespass against thee, go and tell him his fault between thee and him alone: if he shall hear thee, thou hast gained thy brother. But if he will not hear thee, then take with thee one or two more, that in the mouth of two or three witnesses every word may be established. And if he shall neglect to hear them, tell it unto the church: but if he neglect to hear the church, let him be unto thee as an heathen man and a publican."(Matt 18:15-17)

Notice that talking about the individual to someone else is **not** part of God's solution to the problem! Coming home and complaining to our children will not help the problem; it will exacerbate it by poisoning their minds and preventing them from listening to anyone in leadership – including you! Understand that when you pick holes in your authority, be he the boss, the husband, or the pastor, you are picking holes in your own credibility.

I hasten to add here that it is also dangerous to take up your child's side *against* an authority, be it the coach, the Sunday school teacher, or the Christian school teacher. Just because the teacher gives your Johnnie a poor grade doesn't mean the teacher "has it out" for your boy . . . it could be that he actually needs help learning that particular subject. If you could take **a more rational approach and carefully consider all sides of the issue** before passing judgment, it may save you a *lifetime* of heartache.

We will often hold different views than those that are in authority over us. You may disagree with your pastor or other leader about a certain issue—that will happen. It's ok to disagree, but please **do so quietly.** To imply to your children that your pastor, Sunday school teacher, or Christian school teacher is *"clueless"* will detract from his—and ultimately your—credibility in their minds.

God's way of dealing with a problem with *anyone* is to use the pattern given us in Matthew 18, but when we deal with our authorities, we must be careful to be respectful of their position, regardless of their behavior.

> "Render therefore to all their dues: tribute to whom tribute is due; custom to whom custom; fear to whom fear; honour to whom honour."(Romans 13:7)

What can we do if our authorities are not living in a godly manner? Pray, pray, pray!!! And if action is required, do it *quietly, privately*, and *respectfully*.

> "Brethren, if a man be overtaken in a fault, ye which are spiritual, restore such an one in the spirit of meekness; considering thyself, lest thou also be tempted."(Galatians 6:1)

Let's take a worst case scenario for example. We know a family who has four sweet children that they have been trying to raise for God. Both the mother and father love the Lord, and have been very active in church, serving as

Sunday school teachers, etc. But something went wrong—terribly wrong. Through a series of events, it was discovered that the youth director was molesting some of their precious children! It was a parent's worst nightmare.

After the initial shock, anger, and grief, those parents stood up for their children, and that youth director is rightly in prison. He is hopefully in a place where he will not harm anyone anymore.

But what of the young people themselves? Did they lose all respect for anyone in authority and become bitter against God? No, not at all. The last time we saw them, they were productive, happy young people, who are sensitive to the Lord and His leading. And they are still in church, trying to live for God.

If these dear people could take a worst-case scenario and keep it from ruining their children, we can prevent other, and probably less difficult, situations from adversely affecting ours. If we could deal with our disagreements in a rational and Scriptural manner, it would prevent all sorts of troubles, but mostly it would prevent our children from disengaging from a spiritual authority. It's difficult enough for us to have trouble with an authority—let's not let Satan pull a double-whammy on us and use the predicaments to pollute our young people!

I am not advocating blind obedience to a dictatorial leader; I am advocating **sane** and **rational responses to difficulties as they arise.** We are well able to take control of our tongues, thereby taking control of our children's futures.

If there was any way I could impress upon you the importance of this one principle, I would. Our flesh just loves to be justified in our opinions by a multitude of yes-men. But the cost of such a "protective wall" is extreme; it will cost us the souls of our children, who are listening to our every word. Strangely, we feel we are creating a wall of protection of like-minded people while we are really tearing down any defense whatsoever. We are allowing Satan to deceive us, and he will devour our young people, and we will sit and cry, wondering, "What happened? I raised him in church, I taught him the Bible, I sent him to Christian school . . . " They were caught by Satan's deathly claws.

This is reality. It is lifeand death. It is a struggle for your children, and you must be aware of Satan's ploys in order to defend your young people.

I spoke with a first-generation Christian about her two daughters, who are both serving as preacher's wives. "We raised them here in this church," she told me. "And now that they're on their own, they still love their preacher. They think he's one of the best men in the world, and when they come to visit, they always want to see him."

This is exactly what we want to see in our children: a deep-rooted respect for the man of God, and thereby a love and respect for God Himself. As we model to them how to respect authority, they will take our example and live it out for the rest of their lives. The short-term difficulty of keeping our mouth shut can be swallowed up by the long-term blessing of having happy, respectful, godly adult children who love and serve the Lord.

A Deadly Duo

Have you ever blown it with your children? I mean, maybe you got angry and did something you regret. Have you ever thought to yourself, *I really messed up this time! My kids are all going to hate me and grow up to be delinquents!* Maybe you even thought, *How do these other parents seem to raise such happy, godly children? I am so far from perfect, it's hopeless!*

I must admit, when I read parenting books that paint an ideal picture of the model parents, or read about all the things I should be doing, I can get discouraged. It is easy to feel that way. But, when I talked with many second-generation Christians, I discovered a very *encouraging* fact: their parents weren't perfect, either! In fact, one of my respondents very wisely said, **"Those who feel they have all the answers are those who lose their kids."**

> "In your opinion, is it detrimental when parents deal with their children in anger?"

Amen!

One of the most important dynamics that almost every one of my second-generation Christians spoke about was parental anger. It is very significant that *NINETY-SIX percent of my interviewees said that when parents deal with their children in anger, it is detrimental.*

Even in secular circles, parental anger is well known to cause troubles in the family. It comes as no surprise that Satan uses it as a platform for attack. In fact, one of my respondents put it this way, "Anger is very destructive to a child. There are two kinds of anger, good and bad. When we as parents are angry in a good way, it is when we are angry at sin and bad things. But when we become angry toward the young people themselves, it causes wrong discipline and a wrong atmosphere. The spirit of the young person gets hurt, and their pain turns to bitterness."

Another told me how parental anger affected the kids he knew. "For several years," he said, "I ran a college where many of the kids had loads of emotional problems. These kids came from Christian homes, but had all kinds of troubles. Some of them were what I would call spiritually oppressed, and I could say without hesitation that the avenue that Satan used to get into their lives was *bitterness.*"

But, even though the second-generation finds wrathful venting to be harmful to young people, they are quick to add that it is not just expressions of anger alone which causes problems. There is another factor which, when thrown into the mix, can cause a hardening of the heart.

I asked one lady if she knew anyone who is not living for God now, even though he heard the same preaching, and attended the same Christian school. She nodded her head, and without hesitation, identified the cause. She told me, "When a child feels that he's been done an injustice, it seems to fester in his heart, driving a wedge between him and his parents and creating bitterness. I saw it many times with my friends as a young person, and I was tempted sometimes to become bitter against my own parents. As a parent myself now, I realize how important those seemingly "little" injustices are, and when I see my own children struggling with bitterness, I go to them and try to make it right."

She learned from the things she saw that *anger + pride* is **The Deadly Duo.**

> "And, ye fathers, provoke not your children to wrath: but bring them up in the nurture and admonition of the Lord." (Ephesians 6:4).

> "Proud [and] haughty scorner [is] his name, who dealeth in proud wrath." (Proverbs 21:24).

Patterson was again on the hunt. Every night for a week he sat up in a tree like a man possessed. During the day, he tracked, crawled, and tramped through the jungles as though all their lives depended on it ... because they did. Exhaustion seemed to be his constant companion, and he wondered that, tired as he was, if he were to find a lion, would he even be able to take it down? Or would he be the next meal?

Reinforcements of different kinds began to arrive. Many military and civil soldiers, as well as some officers, came to help, each of them staying up night after night in one or another tree, hoping to get a shot at one of the creatures. Amazingly, every couple of nights the lions would manage to elude every single man and trap laid for them and claim another life.

Patterson would later write:

"In the whole of my life I have never experienced anything more nerve-shaking than to hear the deep roars of these dreadful monsters growing gradually nearer and nearer, and to know that some one or other of us was doomed to be their victim before morning dawned. Once they reached the vicinity of the camps, the roars completely ceased, and we knew that they were stalking their prey. Shouts would then pass from camp to camp, "Khabardar, bhaieon, shiataata"

Let me hasten to say that the vast majority of these godly second-generation Christians understood the difference between good anger and bad anger. Many of the people I interviewed feel the same as the one of the assistant pastors I quoted earlier.

In fact, most of my interviewees mentioned that there is a time when it is appropriate to get angry. One young man said, "Just because someone is angry doesn't mean it is sin. I've seen anger in my parents that wasn't wrong; even Jesus was angry at times, especially in the Temple."

A talented church musician, Jennifer, told me, "If a parent expresses anger for the purpose of correction or discipline, then it is helpful rather than harmful. But if the parents are merely releasing frustration, it can cause bitterness and a loss of a desire to communicate, since a child is not sure *what* will set them off."

So we understand from the testimonies of these dear people that an act of purposeful anger may actually be beneficial on occasion—not merely "venting" or "having a short fuse", but expressing displeasure in a forceful, yet deliberate manner—in order to "drive them away" from sin. Having a "short fuse" or a quick temper, however, can cause long-lasting problems. It is the difference between a stick of dynamite that is carefully positioned and detonated to remove an obstacle, or an entire barrel of TNT that blows up indiscriminately and wipes out everything around it.

But sometimes we as parents "blow it". Perhaps we got up on the wrong side of the bed, stubbed our toe, tripped over the cat, and spilled our coffee. That just happens to be the time when Junior comes out of the bedroom with lipstick smeared all over his face! It's the perfect recipe for a violent explosion! Bad days—and sometimes bad responses to them—happen to all of us. Our sin natures combined with circumstances beyond our control sometimes get the best of us!

What did the parents of these godly people do after they lost their temper? Did they pretend it didn't happen and just hope the child understood? No, they faced up to their wrongdoing and were willing to seek the forgiveness of the one they wronged (no matter what their age was.)

This is why the first generation parents I interviewed couldn't seem to express themselves when I asked them how they raised godly children. They know deep down how inadequate they are and how many mistakes they have made. Their understanding of their own sinfulness and realization of their deep need allowed them to walk in humility. Because they needed God's grace, they recognized the fact that they sometimes needed the forgiveness of other people as well, including their children.

Their children, these dear second-generation Christians, also realized that their parents were not perfect—they knew they were imperfect people needing the grace of God.

Dan, a youth pastor with a young wife and new baby, wrote about what he felt was most important in parenting. "I feel that many times young people leave churches because their parents are not transparent with them. In their zeal, the parents try to create the perfect Christian home for their children, and eventually the children begin to realize how planned it is. Parents need to be human beings to their children —capable of making mistakes and messing up."

Giving some significant insights about some of his parents' mistakes, Dan wrote, "My father was saved out of a life of sin and was never taught how to deal with anger. When we were young, he would become angry occasionally;

it was not very fun. However, my dad was very REAL to us, and it enabled me to look past my father's faults. That same anger that he can vividly display when he is frustrated is also used as a topic of comical conversation when our family is together now that we're older! My family was real, and I would say that his realness helped diffuse the tension that his anger caused."

Once again, we see the effect of REALNESS—*imperfection transparent*. We all make mistakes; we cannot hide from them and pretend they don't happen. If we are brave enough to deal with them, those around us will find the strength to learn from our errors.

Lance remarked, "I remember a time when I was nine years old, and my dad got angry with me. He corrected a problem too hastily without verifying, and later discovered that he had made a mistake. But instead of ignoring it, he came back and apologized to me. It was very helpful to me, because I knew I had been dealt with unjustly. Instead of me becoming bitter, his acknowledgement and apology went a long way. My dad was not afraid to apologize when he was wrong, and I learned a big lesson from that."

"I think parental anger greatly affects your kids," Aimee, a young mother, said. "I know when I was growing up, sometimes Mom would get mad, but she would later come back and say, 'Would you forgive me?' I guess I looked up to her more because she did that."

Another second-generation pastor, Scott, wrote me these timely words: "Every child needs to hear a parent say, 'I'm sorry,' whenever the parent has sinned. It shows the child that the parent knows he or she isn't perfect and needs God's grace like all people do."

Dianne, a missionary wife, told me, "Unresolved issues can be points for bitterness to creep in, and in the case of a child, it can be very detrimental. I think sometimes because the parent refuses to humble himself and face the issue, a child will let a root of bitterness creep in, and we all know that a root of bitterness is a chance for the devil to slide in. I don't think a child going to the world happens overnight. I think certain personalities tend to hold resentment, and tend to be more prone to bitterness, and we as parents need to be alert to that."

All of us have sin natures, and everyone gets angry at times. To me, it was a comfort to realize that these faithful parents of godly young people also struggled with the temptation to vent. And sometimes, it got the best of them. Yet, the fact that they didn't allow their pride to keep them from apologizing may have preserved their children.

The people I interviewed told of the difference between good and bad anger, impressed upon me the importance of humility, and then went on to say how their parents handled their feelings. Kevin said, "Sometimes Dad would get angry—and I mean, really, really angry. But he never yelled or did anything rash. He went out the door, got in the car, and went for a drive. He didn't come back until his anger subsided. Some of those drives, though, were looooong ones! But when he came back, he dealt with the situation rationally."

Roland reflected on his childhood, saying, "My dad got angry at us kids sometimes. Looking back, it's a wonder he didn't get angry more often! But when he got angry, he would send us to our rooms until he calmed down enough to deal with the situation properly. He never disciplined us in anger."

Elizabeth remarked, "I rarely saw my parents angry. Sometimes they would get irritated at each other, and then they would go to their bedroom and talk it out. But yelling and screaming just wasn't an option for them."

We can ask the Lord to help us follow the examples of these godly parents by not giving place to our irritation. Allow a little space to cool down when things get hot. Then we can come back to the situation and take care of it wisely.

And if we blow it, we should not be afraid to make things right by humbly apologizing.

The point is, that **Two Wrongs Don't Make a Right**. If we have done wrong by venting our irritation toward our young people, we would be *wrong again* to refuse to humble ourselves and seek their forgiveness. The Bible says,

> Looking diligently lest any man fail of the grace of God; lest any
> root of bitterness springing up trouble you, and thereby many be
> defiled (Hebrews 12:15)

We need to remember that, while our children are yet young, we are to watch for their souls. It is our responsibility to help them deal with the frustrations of life and navigate them through the mazes of difficulties. And sometimes we ourselves are the cause of their frustrations! Even so, we must be ever watchful of those in our care, and seek to sense the real needs of their lives.

> Be thou diligent to know the state of thy flocks, and look well to thy herds. For riches are not for ever: and doth the crown endure to every generation? The hay appeareth, and the tender grass sheweth itself, and herbs of the mountains are gathered. The lambs are for thy clothing, and the goats are the price of the field. And thou shalt have goats' milk enough for thy food, for the food of thy household, and for the maintenance for thy maidens (Proverbs 27:23).

Childhood and youth are not forever. The little blades of tender hay appear in our homes, the young grass pushes up through the earth, and the little lambs are only young for a short time. The Lord has given us this special time in their lives to feed them, strengthen them, and guide them. If we do not look diligently to know the state of those little lambs in our "flock," who will? How are those little lambs? Are they healthy? Do they know they are loved? God has no hands but ours to show them His love. Someday, they will rise up and be a blessing and encouragement to *you.*

> He that delicately bringeth up his servant from a child shall have him become his son at the length. (Proverbs 29:21).

Would you like a son? Bring up a servant *delicately* – carefully, gently, deliberately—and you shall have your son who will love and take care of you the rest of your life. Though we may not be perfect, through God's Grace and by humility, we can prevent our imperfections from adding poison and creating A Deadly Duo.

Always be mindful of the dangers of criticizing authorities, and recognize that anger mixed with pride is equally toxic. These Barriers to a Child's Heart may be just two points, but I think with the Lord's help, we can use these encouraging words to turn our parenting—and even our lives—around so that Satan will not take our children and destroy them in his jaws.

We must do whatever is necessary to help to make them LIONPROOF.

LIONPROOF STRATEGY #10:
DON'T CRITICIZE AUTHORITY!

STRATEGY #11:
WATCH OUT FOR ANGER!

STRATEGY #12:
FREELY ADMIT WHEN YOU ARE WRONG!

PREPARING YOUR DEFENSE:

Carefully examine your children's attitudes toward authority. Do they despise authority, or are they willingly subject? If there is a hint of rejecting authority, take a good, hard look at the way *you* feel about *your* authorities. Many times our children are merely a reflection of us.

Assignment:

1. Carefully study Romans 13 and ask God to give you a proper attitude toward those in authority. If some issue needs to be addressed, remember the admonition in Galatians 6:1: "Brethren, if a man be overtaken in a fault, ye which are spiritual, restore such an one in the spirit of meekness; considering thyself, lest thou also be tempted."

Date completed:_____

2. Are you easily angered? Frustrated? Irritated? Take some time to pinpoint exactly what frustrates you most. It may even be something physical, like a drop in blood sugar levels. Carefully eliminate as many frustration-causing events as possible, and for those that remain, ask God to help you with them.

Below, list the Situation and the possible means of prevention, or way of dealing with the occurrence:

Date completed:_____

Thought Questions for Chapter 11:

1. How was your relationship with your parents when you were a teen? Rocky? Violent? Or peaceful? Why do you think it was that way?

2. Is it possible to have a good relationship with a teenager?

3. What sorts of things do you think teens wonder about? If your young person were to ask you a difficult question, would you be able to answer it?

CHAPTER 11:
NAVIGATING THE TEEN YEARS

One of the mysteries of life: Why is the yappy Chihuahua so eager
to break through the fence to get to the Rottweiler?

*"And when thy son asketh thee in time to come, saying, What mean the
testimonies, and the statutes, and the judgments, which the LORD our
God hath commanded you?*

*Then thou shalt say unto thy son, We were Pharaoh's bondmen in
Egypt; and the LORD brought us out of Egypt with a mighty hand . . .
" Deuteronomy 6:20-21*

****

"In my opinion, Dianne told me, "I think my parents were
not strict enough on us as teenagers especially with the
boyfriend/girlfriend issue. Of course, now that I'm married, I
see how God protected me, but I don't think my parents
quite knew what to do with us when we were teens."

While Dianne spoke (and I typed!) I wondered if any of us really know what we're doing. Yet I was struck by the thought that ignorance is nothing we can afford when our children approach their teens.

How do successful parents handle the teen years? Do they, as I've often heard, put the young person in a barrel when they turn thirteen and take them out again when they turn twenty-one? It may not be a bad idea, but somehow I don't think it will go over very well. There must be some better way to deal with young people.

Thankfully, as I interviewed dozens of second-generation Christians, a pattern began to emerge. There seemed to be common threads in the way the parents of my second-generation respondents handled these children when they were teenagers. These themes popped up regularly as I spoke with these folks, and I think give a very accurate picture of how a parent can handle the difficulties – and the blessings— of the teen years.

Is your young person a "cyoolie?"

Imagine a camp of coolies, but these coolies are modern day teenagers— "cyoolies." Dangers abound when there are teens in the camp because their eyes are open to new things. They look outside the fence, suddenly seeing all kinds of possibilities. They question the fence, wondering, "Why is this here? Is this not an unjust restriction? Look at that great big wonderful jungle out there! Why can't I enjoy it?"

They suspiciously eye the leaders who are prowling about, gun in hand, soberly hunting for lions. To make matters worse, they see themselves as invincible, thinking, "That lion can't get me! I'm fast and strong! I can climb the fence, enjoy life, and crawl back in whenever I please. Others may have gotten killed, but not me."

Cyoolies even have a morbid curiosity with harmful things, while at the same time they hear of folks that have "successfully" gone into danger zones and survived. You can see why the teen years are so dangerous.

It *is possible* to know what we're doing. And it is possible to help our children understand why it is safer in the fence.

Successful parents, and their children, know the answer. And now you will know, too.

As I stated before, many of the successful parents of these second-generation Christians were approachable. This quality alone is extremely vital in the teen years. Young people need someone they can talk to, someone with whom they feel safe. As I was researching this topic on the internet, multitudes of chat rooms dedicated to teens who "need someone to talk to" sprang up. From just a casual glance at this topic, it appears to me that the vast majority of teens rarely consider talking to their parents, and that they instead head to their computers to find someone with whom they can chat. This was not the case with our respondents. They told me of the many times their parents took the time to talk with them and how that influenced their lives (see Chapter 8, Your Most Valuable Weapon.)

Successful Parents Expect Questions

Not only were these parents approachable, but they expected questions from their young people. Teenagers are going through an extremely fluctuating time in their lives and sometimes things pop out of their mouths that even they do not themselves understand. We cannot expect them to be totally rational all the time. In fact, I can't even depend on *me* being totally rational all the time!

Youth is a very formative time, a time for developing beliefs and convictions. When young people reach adulthood, they need to know what they believe and why. Because of these factors, young people will naturally question things. They rarely are trying to hurt the parents; they are merely seeking validation for important issues.

One young lady I quoted before, Shaunna, told how her father understood the spirit of questioning things. She said, "In his mind, our questions were not challenges, they were simply questions wanting to know how or why. If he didn't know the answer, he was honest and told us so."

Questioning helps kids understand what they believe and why.

Cary Schmidt, youth worker since 1990 and author of many books for young people and their parents, says that the ten most common questions teenagers ask are:

1. How do I know what God's will is? How do I know if I'm called to ministry?

2. What's wrong with rock/country/CCM/jazz music? How can you tell what music is good and what is bad?

3. What do you do if you have parents/siblings who are living the wrong way? (one way in church, another way at home, Dad on the internet) How do you avoid wrong influences when you live with them?

4. How do you take a stand with your friends/what do you do when you have a friend that is becoming rebellious?

5. How do you separate from bad friends without hurting them or making them think you're stuck up? How can I be a witness to my friends and still be accepted?

6. What's wrong with holding hands, kissing, etc., before marriage?

7. Why is it so hard to be consistent in the Christian life as a teenager?

8. Why are we supposed to dress differently/wear non-worldly clothes? (What is appropriate and modest clothing and why?)

9. What's wrong with going to the movies? (and other issues of separation)

10. How do you get over/deal with a broken relationship (dating & friendships)?

He goes on to say:

> These questions reveal a lot of real life issues and a strong desire to know "why" or "how." As adults, we ignore this list to our own detriment. This is what our young adults are seeking to understand. This is what has them tied up in knots. This is what holds them back spiritually, emotionally, etc. Thankfully, God's Word has answers to every issue—and it's up to us to apply His truth and make it come alive.[38]

Almost any and all questions young people ask, even if they ask them in a wrong manner or a seemingly critical spirit, prove that they are thinking deeply about life's issues and are seeking to find the answers to them. We cannot afford to ignore their questions! Rather, expect them. Successful parents did, and now that you know how important it is, you will anticipate them too.

Successful Parents Respond Rationally

In addition to expecting questions, our *response* to questions is vastly important, as well. How should we answer when our young people ask questions? Certainly, we should try to prepare in advance for their questions. The Bible says in 1 Peter 3:15:

> "But sanctify the Lord God in your hearts: and be ready always to give an answer to every man that asketh you a reason of the hope that is in you with meekness and fear:"

Also, we must:

> "Study to shew thyself approved unto God, a workman that needeth not to be ashamed, rightly dividing the word of truth."(2 Timothy 2:15).

How wonderful it would be if we could take the time while our children are young to prepare ourselves for the inevitable questions they will have when they are older! Often, however, their questions catch us off guard.

Many times we don't have the answers yet. What should we do? We should tell them honestly that we don't know, but we will look into it. Meanwhile, we should be careful to ***maintain an attitude of approachability.*** Remember, if we push them away, we are in danger of pushing them into the arms of someone who will give them wrong guidance. At the very least, pushing away our young people when they come to us for answers will slowly but surely kill our relationship with them.

Aimee, a middle-aged mother, said, "My mom was approachable, but not really my dad. Dad seemed to think we were gossiping every time we came to him with a problem or a question about someone. I got rebuffed over and over, and eventually I quit talking to him. We have a very detached relationship at this point. It's really kind of sad."

But it doesn't have to be this way. We can allow our young people to ask us questions, or perhaps even encourage them to. The questions are there, burning deep in their soul. They will ask someone. God helping us, it should be Mom and Dad.

Steve told me, "Mom always wanted to keep us close. As I was growing up, my dad was very busy, and Mom did a lot of things that kept us close. She read books, and even recorded them on tape for us when we couldn't be together. In our home, Daddy was law, and Momma was grace. I'm very thankful I had a good relationship with my parents. I knew I could talk to them about anything."

For more on this subject, see the chapter on Having Your Child's Heart.

Often as parents, we feel threatened by our children's questions. Whether we fear that they are going to head down the same slippery slope we were on as young people, or whether we fear that they are going to ruin our reputation (especially if we are in the ministry), we need to be careful to understand that their questions usually are not as earth-shaking as they sound. Young people have a tendency to blurt out their comments in the most unbecoming manner sometimes! They are just coming to grips with their own emotions, and trying to find the best way (or even the best time) to ask a question is generally not something they think about very much.

As you examine the issues your young person struggles with, take the time to patiently teach them to present their questions as actual questions, rather than demands or challenges. Remind them that you are always ready and willing to help them, but that it would be a help to you if they could frame their questions in an overly emotional and perhaps non-confrontational manner.

Herein lies the key: taking the time to pass on your values in a casual environment. Perhaps during family devotions, you can gradually deal with a sensitive subject, or during a family meal. Even while you are fishing you can drop little bits of information you have gleaned concerning an important issue. The key is to keep discussions upbeat, short, and informative, until the young person becomes comfortable listening to you and talking to you, and ultimately understanding your values.

Successful Parents Taught Their Young People the Reasons Behind the Rules!

(See Chapter 6: Building A Barricade, and Chapter 7: Maintaining a Consistent Vigil)

Remember how the people I spoke to understood why they were sheltered? They not only understood why, but eventually embraced the values their parents taught them, and now they themselves are sheltering their own children. The parents took the time to explain the rules, and the reasons behind them, in a rational, casual manner, and in a happy, relaxed atmosphere.

Many times the queries of a young person will force us to analyze our beliefs. This analyzing is a good thing, if it ultimately reinforces the Biblical reasons for what we do and why. However, sometimes the questioning can cause parents to go into a tail spin. If the parents don't really have very good reasons why they do what they do, they can be swayed by the opinions and questions of the young people. Of course, when the parents give in to the young people, it then sets the stage for an "anything goes" sort of atmosphere. This is never good for the family.

For a few weeks, there was relative calm. It seemed as though perhaps the lions had gone elsewhere.

"He's got to be gone, this time for good!" one of the men declared. Several of the coolies nodded their heads in agreement. One looked at Patterson, and stopped. The colonel's eyes were fire. "He's not gone, not by a long shot. Men, take all the precautions you can – he will be back!"

The coolies didn't need any more prodding. They had been through many an uncomfortable night as they slept in odd makeshift beds out of lion-reach. They would continue to live in discomfort, if only it meant that they could continue to live.

It was a good thing, because one thickly clouded night, he did come back. Patterson's scalp prickled as he heard men yelling, "The lion! He's back! He's trying to get me!" He closed his eyes and shook his head. There was very little he could do, for he knew the entire area was completely shrouded in darkness. In a mad attempt to frighten the monster, he took his rifle and fired several shots into the air. Amazingly, his plan worked. Not one man was lost that night.

One mother wrote me of a friend of hers whose fifteen year old girl was straining at the bit to leave home. "She just pesters and pesters and pesters to wear whatever she wants," the friend told her. "We've always tried to have our children dress more conservatively, but all she wants to wear is immodest clothes. In fact, she's obsessed with it! She can't wait to leave the house so she can wear what she wants."

The mother wrote that, a few weeks after that conversation, the girl was wearing immodest clothing to a youth outing, and within another few weeks, she was wearing her immodest clothing to church. The girl finally got what she wanted, and was able to wear whatever she wished...all because her parents gave in to her "questions," which turned into demands, and eventually an expressed desire to leave the home . . . otherwise known as a threat. It is a progression, or rather a regression, which occurs every time parents compromise on a rule for their home which they had held for so long.

The moral of the story?

- Don't establish a rule that you are not willing to keep and enforce throughout your life.

- Set your rules very carefully, prayerfully, and STICK TO THEM.

- Teach them to your children, and

- Tell them the WHY behind the rules.

- Expect questions, but have a ready answer.

Don't let questioning cause you to waver from something the Lord has given you.

Successful parents understand that some lines will be crossed.

Several of the young people I talked to told me what their parents did when they crossed a line. I found the response of the parents to be interesting, and telling at the same time.

Before the line is crossed, parents need to decide in advance what their response would be. Without having clear lines and definite responses, things are up for grabs. Like we said before, children do not need an "anything goes" atmosphere in the home.

I learned this principle while talking to one of the people I interviewed awhile back.

James told me, "My sister had this thing with wanting to wear clothes she knew my parents did not approve of. Her way of wearing my parents down was unusual. She timed herself so that she would just about make us late for church, and then would come out wearing something that she knew Dad would not approve of. Of course, by this time, Dad was really in a hurry. You could see the frustration and irritation building up in him. Finally, though, he just waved his hand and said, 'Oh, come on, we've got to go!' And my sister got her way. This became the normal way things went at our house. And you know what? My sister is living away from God and out of church to this day. Perhaps if Dad had taken the time to make sure she did what she was supposed to, she might be in church today."

Since then, I've heard many such stories, and they are all sad. These tales can never have a happy ending, for *a life lived straining against authority can never be happy.* Let's not doom our children to a wasted life; don't let Satan catch them in his claws. Let's do whatever is necessary to make them LIONPROOF.

Successful Parents Take Swift and Decisive Action.

One young assistant pastor told of a three month period of rebellion he had when he was seventeen. He got in with the wrong crowd, perhaps because of work, and began listening to rock music, which pushed him further into rebellion. He said, "I would listen to rock music in my truck, and then switch the channel before I got out, so that if Dad got in and checked the radio, he wouldn't know what I was listening to. Besides, he was having some physical troubles, so I figured he wouldn't bother checking. Well, one day I forgot to change the channel before I got out, and Dad checked it. He turned on the radio and heard this blaring rock music, and his heart broke. But with Dad, he also had a bit of holy anger, and he tore that radio right out of my truck and smashed it on the ground, right beside the truck, so that when my friends and I came out after school, we would all see the broken pieces and know we'd been caught. Then he left a post-it note on the dashboard which read, "Now I know why I'm having heart trouble." That was all he said. But he didn't need to say another word; I knew I had broken his heart and caused him physical distress. It broke my heart, too, and because of that, I got right with my parents, and also with God."

We can conclude that it is important to respond more severely when rebellion is involved. And if you have a strong relationship with your child, the results are much more likely to be positive for both of you.

Some parents will deal strenuously when their young person crosses a line, while others respond calmly and deliberately. One example of the effectiveness of the latter response was given to me by Steve, who remarked how he backslid from God for a short time:

His story is quoted earlier, in Chapter 8, "Your Most Valuable Weapon." You'll remember that his mother was very frank with him, and told him, "Steve, I didn't raise you to serve the Devil." The strength of her relationship with him is what enabled her to be so bold.

The teen years need not be turbulent ones, though they may be difficult. With God's help, we can expect questions, respond rationally, teach the reasons behind the rules, understand that some lines will be crossed, and take swift and decisive action. We can make the right decisions and set our lines carefully. The Lord will help us stick to the decisions we've prayed about . . . the ones He Himself has given us. God is not willing for Satan to catch any of our young people in his claws! It is not only possible, but necessary, to make them LIONPROOF!

LIONPROOF STRATEGY # 13:

EXPECT QUESTIONS AND PREPARE FOR THEM!

Preparing Your Defense:

1. I hate to sound like a broken record, but do your children know the rules in your home? Do they realize and understand the consequences of breaking a rule? Again, be CLEAR and consistent.

2. Knowing that swift and consistent responses to rule-breaking are crucial, determine that you will do whatever is necessary to respond appropriately. Be willing to make some life-style changes by turning off electronics or removing other distractions so you are able to recognize when a line is crossed.

3. Carefully evaluate how you treat each child. Keep the rules consistent from child to child. If you didn't allow your firstborn to do a particular activity when he is ten years old, don't allow the youngest to do it when he reaches the same age, either.

ASSIGNMENT:

1. If you haven't already done so, work with your spouse to create a list of your core family values. As you make the list, take your Bible and support each point with Scripture. This will create a strong backbone for your family as your children approach their teen years.

    Date completed: _____

2. Try to answer, from the Scriptures, each question that teens are likely to ask (see Cary Schmidt's list, quoted earlier in the chapter.) Determine which questions will need more study, and then take the time to slowly and methodically, with prayer, seek answers to those questions. These are questions young people need answers for, so you may as well prepare!

    Date completed:_____

Thought Questions for Chapter 12:

1. How can you prepare your young people to stand alone in real life?

2. Does the "letting go" process affect a young person's early adulthood? How?

3. In your own observations, why do you think so many young people go to the world as soon as they are able?

CHAPTER 12:
HITTING THE MARK—
HOW SUCCESSFUL PARENTS
LAUNCHED THEIR CHILDREN

"Making the decision to have a child is momentous. It is to decide forever to have your heart go walking around outside your body." –Elizabeth Stone[39]

"As arrows are in the hand of a mighty man; so are children of the youth." Psalm 127:4

****

*After the first lion's demise, the hunter's thoughts turned to his coolies. They were his charge, his precious responsibility. Quietly he stole through the jungle, knowing dangers were everywhere. The sobering realization came to him that even when – or if – he could kill the second lion, th*ere would be other lions, *perhaps even other dangers which lurked in the jungle. He knew that one day his job would be over, and he would have to leave. How would he prepare his charges to slay their own lions? As he continued his trek, his mind drifted toward a story he had read long ago....*

****

THE TALE OF FOUR ARCHERS

Once there were four archers. They had spent years preparing their arrows for the Great Tournament—sharpening them, preening them, and training them. The years have passed so fast, and now it is time to put the arrows to the test and let them go.

The first archer steps up to the shooting line, and carefully nocks his arrow, setting it on the string. He raises his strong arms, draws back his bow, aims, and . . . continues to stand there, ready, poised. But nothing happens. His completely prepared arrow stays on his bow and remains ineffective.

The second archer steps up, and prepares to shoot. His arrow has been his pride and joy, and he is clearly nervous. Has he worked on it enough? Is it really ready? What if it misses the mark? His sinking gloom pervades the already tense atmosphere. With his arrow ready, he takes aim, and releases. Immediately something is terribly wrong. His arrow begins going astray. Fury arises in his heart, and he begins to yell at his arrow, criticizing it, ordering it to get back in line. The arrow wobbles, and continues to stray. The archer stomps and calls his arrow terrible names, belittling him. "I KNEW you'd never amount to anything!" he yells. The arrow wobbles into the grass, and the archer turns his face away, muttering under his breath.

The third archer steps up, and prepares his arrow to shoot. He has an air of unconcern as he raises his arm, and shoots without even aiming! Incredibly, as soon as the arrow leaves the bow, the third archer turns away and goes about his own life. The arrow finds its own way and gets lost in the woods.

The fourth archer prepares his arrow to shoot. His confidence is noticeable, and he speaks calmly to his arrow, smiling, and patting it. He has loved this arrow, sheltered this arrow, trained his arrow, worked alongside his arrow, and spent his life for his arrow. It is time now for his arrow to go and hit the mark. He sets his arrow on the string, raises his strong arms, draws back the bow and . . .

****

Letting go of our children is one of the hardest parts of parenting. After all, when they are under our roof, we know what's going on in their lives and can provide guidance when they need it. But to let go is to allow our children to take over the control of their own lives and make their own decisions. It is a nerve-wracking time; we realize that soon it will be apparent whether or not we parents have done our job.

Some of the most significant advice I heard on Letting Go was while talking to the younger second-generation Christians. Their experiences, and those of their friends, are still new and fresh in their minds, unclouded by the whirl of activity surrounding growing families. They remember clearly the process they went through as they were launched from their homes, and the experiences of their friends as well.

The Death Grip

The Death Grip is the way that some of our respondents' friends were launched. It takes on many forms, but the results are the same: the young person is gripped almost to a strangle-hold, and then suddenly released to live on his own with little or no preparation. Understand that *sheltering is not the problem*; the problem lies in the fact that many parents simply do not prepare their young people to live in a world full of sin and vice.

Shaunna, a twenty-six year old daughter of a missionary, told me about some of the young people with whom she attended college. "As a homeschooled kid," she said, "I was sheltered from worldly influences, but I know that a gradual letting go is very important. I attended a college which is made up of predominantly homeschoolers, many of whom came from a sheltered environment. It seemed that many of them were unprepared for their newly found freedom and the worldly influences they were suddenly surrounded by. *They* were the ones that went into a tailspin. Strangely enough, it seemed that those who had some contact with the world growing up did better with their freedoms."

Now, I personally recognize the importance in this day and age to keep our young ladies safe from those who would take advantage of them. That is why my husband and I feel that our girls should go seamlessly from their father's house to their husband's house. But within their father's house, there must be a way that a young lady will be useful, will feel needed, will have some freedom, and will be able to contribute to their own and their families' welfare.

Young men also need to be sheltered. This world is full of wickedness and sin, and our young men should be able to approach adulthood with clean minds and pure hearts. But keeping them locked up at home is not the answer; they must be prepared to deal with the lure of the world. (See The Guiding Hand, this chapter)

Yes, the world has a terrible pull, but there is no need for a death grip, or for panic. As we follow the Lord and His plan for our lives and the lives of our young people, we will be successful! By God's grace and with His help, they can be LIONPROOF.

Hands Off!

The Hands Off method of Letting Go is the way your average American is launched. It is also the way your average young person in a Christian home is raised. There is a philosophy pervading in America, and in the world, that we should just let young people go their own way, and they'll find their useful place in society. The parents don't provide support, encouragement, or guidance. They launch their children and turn away to their own lives, leaving the young people to sort life out on their own. It's a dangerous and difficult way to live.

And then, some people even have a Hands-Off philosophy all through their young person's childhood!

Some also have differing philosophies for different children, treating their youngest (or favorite) child in a Hand's Off way. Though I mentioned some of these things before (see Chapter 8: Maintaining a Consistent Vigil,) they bear repeating, since these points were brought up numerous times by my respondents.

Some people shelter their children while they are young, and then loosen their guidance during the teen years. One lady told of how her parents seemed to show favoritism to her sister. "I don't know why," she explained, "but they seemed to let her get away with more. Maybe it's because she is younger, or because they got older, but the rules were different with her than they were with me. And with her, they gave her freedoms I never had. It had a detrimental effect on her. She seemed to focus on just "having fun," and after she got married, when marriage was no longer 'fun.' she got out of it. Now it's awful the crazy things she's involved in, all for 'fun.' But it's a hard life, Lisa. A real hard life. She pays dearly for her 'fun.'"

Letting up on a child as they get older can be just as detrimental as treating one child differently than another, or perhaps more so. When there is consistency in enforcement of the rules all through childhood, even if there are very few rules, children seem better prepared to face adulthood.

The Hands Off approach does little for raising godly children, and for launching them, as our respondents aptly tell us.

The Guiding Hand

On the other hand (pun intended!), the vast majority of our respondents were sheltered and received guidance from their parents as they were growing up. Jennifer told me about how her mother maintained a good relationship with her, even while she was away at college. "Because I have a disability," she said, "I have a very hard time finding clothes that fit me just right. I was really busy at college, and had a low time when I was desperate for some clothes and had zero time to sew. My physical troubles were also a constant challenge, and I had a difficult time battling with depression. One day a package arrived in my mailbox, and it was a special package from Mom. Inside, there was a carefully sewn skirt which fit me beautifully, and a precious note which I still have to this day. She wrote, 'I just wanted you to know, that every stitch was sewn with love and prayer. I love you!' That little gesture of love and concern got me through the rest of my college days. I knew Mom was there for me.

As we have seen in the chapter 8: Your Most Valuable Weapon, it is through a strong relationship that values are transferred. Simply put, if our children know we love them, they will more readily accept our guidance.

Also, the vast majority of respondents had regular contact with the world through a consistent church outreach program. These young people were either raised in the ministry, or very involved in church activities. (Sixty-four percent of my respondents were raised in the ministry as opposed to "regular" homes.) Even at a young age, many of them—especially those who were raised working in the bus ministry reaching often-neglected children—saw first-hand the effects of poor decision-making in the families they helped reach. They saw the heartbreak and difficulty those poor decisions made on the families, and especially the children who get shuffled from one parent to another. The sad lifestyles they saw proved to them that "the way of the transgressor is hard." For those second-generation Christians, choosing to live for God seemed a much better alternative.

By contrast, those young people who did the worst when they reached adulthood were those who were very sheltered all their life, AND had rocky or non-existent relationships with their parents, and who were then released to the world without any guidance other than, "because I said so!" They viewed their new-found freedom as something different and interesting. Many found their way into the waiting jaws of the prowling lion, Satan.

Those that did the best were those that had regular, monitored contact with the world through evangelism. In addition, they were introduced incrementally to the world, and provided with support and guidance all through the process.

Generally speaking, our respondents were allowed increasing measures of controlled freedom as they increased in responsibility.

Then, when they were on their own, their parents continued to give support and advice when asked. Letting go is natural, and it provides an opportunity for both parent and child to continue to grow. Steve's words are again helpful to us: "My parents have not stopped parenting just because we are all out of the house. It's not that they have the rule over us, but they still have a part in our lives. They're interested in my burdens and keeping me close to them and to the Lord."

While many theories abound as to the best way to Let Go of our young people, those that have experienced the Guiding Hand are by far the most likely to continue to serve God when they are out on their own. May we as parents learn from their experience not to hold our children with the Death Grip, or the opposite error, not to hold them at all (the Hands Off method).

****

The arrow of the fourth archer sped through the air, spurred onward by his cheering squad which he could plainly hear behind him. "Go, buddy, go, go!" the archer's voice carried through the air. "You can do it! I know you can hit the mark and be something for the Lord! You're doing great! Oh, how I love you! I am so proud of you!" Setting his face with determination, the young arrow sped through the air, knowing in his heart that THIS was why he was made —THIS was his purpose for living. His life's purpose came fully into view, and he allowed neither leisure nor sin to deter him from his life's calling. The feeling of purpose so overwhelmed him that he could not help but give his all to hit the mark. With the precision of a surgeon's knife, the arrow sliced right into the very center of the target, and he heard a great cheer arise from behind him. And the feeling that soared through his heart when he had fulfilled his purpose was so exhilarating that he could only say, "Thank you, God, for a mom and dad who loved me, encouraged me, and believed in me. I love you!"

****

The next evening, the colonel again took up his position. Slowly, the moon crept up the cloudless sky, giving Patterson a clear view of all around. During his gun-bearer's watch, the colonel slept fitfully, but awoke with the eerie feeling that something was terribly wrong. Glancing over at his gun-bearer, he saw that he was not aware of anything unusual. Still, Patterson just had a . . . feeling. That's it! *he thought.* It's quiet . . . too quiet. *Scanning the jungle intensely, Patterson could see nothing unusual, and after a time was about to close his eyes again when he saw it: a great shadowy figure coming closer.*

The man-eater was stalking them.

Wasting no time, Patterson fired off a round right at the lion's chest. With a dull thud, the shot hit the beast, and a savage growl tore the air. He didn't fall, however, but bounded toward the jungle, seeking refuge, but not before Patterson could fire a volley of shots his direction. Another loud growl told the colonel that one of them had hit its mark.

As soon as the early morning became light enough, Patterson and two companions, a native tracker and a gun-bearer, easily followed the trail of blood. A vicious snarl shocked the party, and the enraged lion broke through the trees and began to charge. Patterson fired his gun, but in spite of the fact that each bullet hit its mark, the beast kept on coming. Having no more ammunition, the colonel put out his hand for the Martini rifle his gun-bearer carried, but both the man and the weapon had disappeared up the nearest tree, leaving Patterson alone with a charging wounded lion and no weapon.

Taking a massive leap, the colonel barely scrambled up the same tree in time. The beast was about to flee again into the jungle when Patterson grabbed the Martini from his gun-bearer and shot once more into the giant. There was a loud thud as his body hit the ground, and all was silent. Finally he was dead…or was he? The colonel slid down the tree to check on his kill.

He didn't realize that the monster was still alive.

Carelessly, Patterson approached the brute. All of a sudden, the lion leaped up and attacked! Thankfully the colonel still had his rifle, and he quickly shot a sixth bullet into the lion's chest. Another bullet to the head finished off the second man-eater not five yards from the colonel. The lion died, biting a branch and clawing the ground.

And this time he *was* dead.

LIONPROOF STRATEGY # 14:
LET THEM GO WITH A GUIDING HAND...
...BUT DO LET THEM GO!

Preparing Your Defense:

1. Do you know anyone who held their young person with a Death Grip? How did that situation turn out?

2. Certainly you know many young people who were raised with the Hands Off method. Did those young people fare any better?

Assignment:

1. Pray together with your spouse about how to best incrementally introduce your child to the world. Plan some activities that will put him, for brief periods, in contact with those who live a different lifestyle. Afterwards, talk with him, ask him questions, and give him some guidance.

2. Determine in your heart that you will do all you can to continue to develop a close relationship to your young person. Evaluate each of your children. What do they enjoy? What do they dislike? How do they express love? (You may want to read a very good and useful book, *The Five Love Languages for Children* for some ideas here.) Using the answers you receive, reach out to your young person on a regular basis.

Child's Name	What do they enjoy? (activity, book, etc.)	What do they dislike? (try to avoid these)	How do they show love? (try to express love to them the way they perceive love)

Date Completed:_____

PART FOUR

THE EXCEPTIONS

Now, let us turn from the untouched survivors, and see another group. This group is somehow different from the rest. They have been here all this time, working and serving faithfully, but we have hardly noticed them.

We draw closer, and as we do, we see one who is missing her foot. Her bearing is regal, however, and it is with surprise that we notice her disability.

Our eyes see another—and we realize that his features are so marred, we can hardly resist staring. But he is conversing with such ease and confidence, and his smile is disarming, so we move even closer.

Another lady gracefully approaches the group, tray in hand, and smiles at each one, offering a refreshing glass of water. She seems thrilled to serve the others, yet as she turns, we are shocked to see that she is missing a hand! But she handles the tray with ease.

These are the exceptions.

Marred by the lions, but alive, thankful, and useful . . .

And this is their story.

No thought questions,

No assignments,

Just read,

...and *think*.

CHAPTER 13:
THE EXCEPTIONS

Spiritual Abuse

Shortly after beginning my interview with Rod, I knew he was different. I asked, "How many generations back can you trace your Christian heritage?"

His intense gaze gave increased meaning to his words. With emphasis, he replied, "I am a fourth-generation preacher *by the grace of God.*" After he answered a few more questions, I realized that there was something terribly wrong with his upbringing. My pen paused in midair as my heart wrenched. *He is right! He really is a fourth-generation preacher* <u>by the grace of God</u>.

Though most people I've talked to fall into a fairly predictable pattern, there were a very few who didn't. These people are those I call The Exceptions. They are second-generation Christians who are serving the Lord *in spite* of something (or many somethings) that happened to them in their childhood. They are The Overcomers, and they have, by the grace of God, prevailed to live for Jesus though they experienced something that would have waylaid many other people.

Several of the people I interviewed had a childhood which I would consider Emotionally Abusive, Caustic, or perhaps even Spiritually Abusive, since the parents used spiritual things to browbeat the children. It is a warped form of Christianity, which is not a real form of Christianity at all. However, the parents put on such a good front that one lady I spoke with said, "People come up to me and tell me what a blessing my mother has been to them, and how godly she is. I just nod my head numbly, but my heart breaks . . . if only they knew the horror I had to live through at home."

It is a heinous crime against God and against children, and it needs to be exposed for what it is: wickedness.

For the most part, I will let these people tell their stories, but I have identified some common factors which make this form of toxic parenting recognizable. God help all of us to avoid these dangerous parenting practices!

- Mother is in charge, and Father is weak

"My dad was a pastor, and then a missionary. He knew how to raise godly kids, but in all reality, Mom was in charge. My parents had a rocky marriage, but it's a lot better now than it used to be, strangely enough—now that Dad's come into line with Mom. Biblically speaking, the marriage is actually very poor."

- Mother is obsessed with being spiritual

"My parents, especially my mother, were always trying to be the most spiritual, but their spirituality was very superficial. They took us to good, solid churches, and we heard good preaching. We had so many saved relatives, we even had our own family camp meeting. Devotions in our home were routinely an hour long."

"My mother would often stand up in church and give "testimonies" – twenty minute sermonettes, complete with three points and a challenge at the end. That is, until she had two nervous breakdowns. I would guess that *she was unable to handle the stress of always trying to be right*. Now her speech is affected, and she is unable to give her 'testimonies.'"

- Discipline is unusually severe and harsh

"There was little, if any, mercy when we kids did something wrong. My parents loved me—I guess—but the only way they showed it was through severity—although my mom seemed to have some strange desire for us to show her affection in public, probably to help her look good. Regardless, the mode of discipline was very harsh."

"One time I remember I misunderstood a command. I was eleven at the time, and I thought they had just given us a suggestion. Because I misunderstood what they said, I was given fifty whacks! My home would be what I would consider harsh—many rules which were very strictly enforced."

- Extreme Desire to Look Good

"My parents were always trying to be the most spiritual, but their standards were very inconsistent. It seemed to me that it was a worse offense to do something in front of the church folks than it was to do the same thing at home. Their main desire was to maintain their image, and if anyone saw through their façade, they talked about that person and ran them into the ground.

"We were always a very musical family, and we did a lot of singing together in the different churches and in the big camp meetings. Everybody thought we were such a wonderful family, but they didn't know what it was like behind closed doors.

"My parents were never faithful or loyal to anyone, but would always talk about those they didn't agree with. At the first sign of trouble, they bailed out. We moved a lot, eventually attending somewhere around seventeen or eighteen different churches, because, of course, my parents could never find one they could agree with. Or they were "found out" for what they were. Every time they left a church, they were always the 'victim.'"

- Emphasis Placed Solely on the Outward

"Their emphasis was always placed on the outward appearance—what we as Christians do and what we don't do. Of course, the list of what we *couldn't* do was much longer than the list of what we *could* do. As I was growing up, I knew the list, but I was not saved; I had no idea why I was doing those things. (*See Ch. 11, Navigating the Teen Years*)

"In our home, standards were a badge of honor, a feather in your cap."

- Love is Based on Performance

LISA B. RAUB

"My mother seemed to crave attention. She would hug and kiss us, but mostly just to fulfill some need of her own to be loved. She would love only on her own terms—that was if you made her look good in front of others. Often we were forced to hug her in public. It made me, as a teenager, feel very uncomfortable."

- Worry and Manipulation Seemed to Be The Mode of Dealing With Problems

"My folks did a lot of worrying. They also did a lot of talking about anyone they didn't agree with. Though my dad rarely complained, Mom did a lot of complaining; it seemed like she was rarely happy with anything!

"As for physical or financial troubles, we didn't know about too many of them; they sheltered us quite a bit from that. But as far as relationships are concerned, they always blamed others, and manipulated things to try to fix the situation."

There are some points that I think are very important. Rod mentioned several times that anger was a big issue in his home. He said, "One of the most hideous things I experienced is something I still see all the time. There are angry mothers—domineering and power hungry mothers—mothers who are strangely warped in their spirituality. I see hen-pecked fathers who cannot stand up to the spiritual manipulation of their wives, and who sit passively while their family rides the spiritual wave right to Hell.

"It's a perverted role, with the woman in charge, giving all the orders, and the man being the kind, passive one. Those perverted roles produced sodomy; in fact, my sister is now a lesbian.

"I've seen in my experience as a fourth-generation Christian and now as a pastor myself: Daddy MUST be in charge, and Momma must be submissive. If the family doesn't operate that way, it is a dysfunctional family.

"One of the most important things I learned from my childhood is to be REAL—don't try to be super-spiritual in front of other people, and something else at home. That kind of life is complete insanity.

"Another thing I learned is the importance of apologizing. As a parent, I must be careful to apologize when I'm wrong. I should not always think I'm right just because I'm the parent, or that I know what I'm doing when I really don't. I've found that to be completely destructive."

One of the young men I interviewed, whom I will call Travis, joined the Marine Corps "to get away from all the rules." (!!!) During his tenure there, he experienced the grace of God in a very unusual way. Though he was a born-again Christian, deep down he wasn't sure if his parents' Christianity was for him. At some point, the Lord revealed to him **that the errors of his parents did not have to be his own.** His testimony is riveting. I'll merely quote from him:

"While I was in the Marine Corps, I remember one time being in a conference room with a high-ranking colonel while he received a call from the Major General in Iraq. The officer in Iraq asked the Colonel an extremely important question about an upcoming mission, the mission to take a certain hill. The Colonel spoke vehemently into the phone, "My question is not 'can we win,' because I know my Marines can win, but my question is, 'Is that hill worth my boys *dying* upon right *now*? We know we can win, but maybe we need to wait a week, or bomb it some more. Maybe we need to wait a few months and barrage it. But is that hill worth *dying* on **now**?"

"It struck me with such force that I was literally frozen to the spot. Suddenly I realized that during my childhood my parents made battles out of every tiny little hill, and *we children were the casualties.*

"Somehow I am serving the Lord today, but in reality it is not because of my upbringing, it is in spite of it."

Parents, pick your battlefields very carefully...prayerfully! Remember, Satan loves battlefields. While the family is lobbing missiles at each other, attacking each other with m16s and bayonets, they are not vigilant for the more dangerous attack – the attack from Satan. Their distraction provides perfect cover for him to **mark his chosen delicacy**, and **come in** and *catch his prey.* Don't let your child be taken.

Careful, prayerful consideration of our actions goes a long way to keeping our children from the claws of the Devil and helping them be LIONPROOF.

Successful Parents	Caustic Parents
Biblical roles—Father in charge, Mother supportive and submissive	Mother in charge, Father weak
Both parents really, truly love God with all their heart	Parents obsessed with being outwardly spiritual
Discipline is consistent, rational	Discipline is unusually severe and harsh
Extreme desire to please God out of love	Extreme desire to look good
Emphasis placed on the heart, and the outward follows	Emphasis placed solely on the outward
Love is unconditional	Love based on performance
Problems dealt with through praying and trusting God	Problems dealt with through worry and manipulation

Sexual Abuse

Every kind of abuse carries its own horror, but sexual abuse is perhaps one of the most damaging. Though Debi's father, a pastor, and her mother were careful to shelter her, they had no idea that perverts abound even in conservative churches. Satan was able to creep in through a gap in the defense. Unfortunately, it is a gap which is very common, but very dangerous.

As I interviewed, Debi, who was a missionary's wife, I thought about how her story is so horrifying, but her healing so miraculous.

I will merely allow her to tell her story.

> My parents were very careful to try to shelter me from explicit things on TV, or other places, and any time the subject was brought up, it was quickly hushed. It was a forbidden subject in our home.

Abuse occurred by a trusted relative, on church property

> When families got together and the parents wanted to talk without the children bothering them, they would send us children off to a bedroom to play.
>
> It was during this time that my older cousin began sexually abusing me, and this occurred in empty Sunday school rooms after church. In the beginning as I was so young, I thought was some sort of secret game. I didn't realize how awful this "game" was. Strangely, whenever this was going on, my parents were just in the next room, completely oblivious to the wickedness that was going on.
>
> As the abuse continued through the years I carried a heavy weight of guilt that drove me to suicide attempts as a teenager. Did my parents ever ask me the question, "Has anyone ever done this to you . . . ?" They sure did, and so did the psychiatrist, but I never told them.
>
> As a teenager I started to despise my parents but I hated myself most of all. I tried so many things to make the guilt go away. Cutting [my wrists] seemed to make me feel better.

I was obsessed with suicidal thoughts and wanted to die so badly. Finally, someone came along who seemed to understand—our new youth director. Everyone loved him. We had waited so long for someone to take over the youth department.

Trusted youth directors, pastors, or church leaders may not be so trustworthy

One day the youth director asked me to babysit his toddler daughter for a week. His wife didn't know. She worked nights and slept during the day, and she was surprised to see me at her house (with her husband) when she came home from work. The youth director's office (at his secular job) was right next door to his house, but he hardly went to "work".

I must say that when the youth director came to pick me up that first morning my mom had a bad feeling as we drove away. **If only** she would have gone with her intuition or the Lord's leading and came and gotten me, or prevented me from going the rest of the week! It wasn't until Thursday when he made his move.

With his wife in the next room asleep, he attempted to sexually assault me. The worst part about it is that when confronted about it the entire church took his side. Of course, he denied everything! They said, "Either he is the best actor on the planet, or you are lying."

Debi had no one to turn to and was trapped in her situation. Only the grace of God kept her from suicide. She managed to survive her high school years, and attended Bible college, but the weight of guilt and bitterness simply wouldn't leave. It wasn't until she realized she truly hadn't trusted the Lord for her soul's salvation that she found the peace, love, and forgiveness for which she had been searching. Though she had made many professions of faith over the years, she was not truly saved. She had grown up in a pastor's home, taught Sunday school herself, worked with children to lead them to Christ, and even attended Bible College. At nineteen years of age, she found forgiveness . . . she found Christ.

It is only by the grace of God that I am serving the Lord! Jesus made me a new creature—therefore I experienced a genuine change in my life.

Suddenly, life took on a new meaning for Debi. She became electrified with the thought that the Lord still loved her and was not angry at her. In fact, He could even use her past to glorify Himself!

Remember what Joseph went through? Yet he said: *"But as for you, ye thought evil against me; but God meant it unto good . . . " (Genesis 50:20a).* I couldn't help but think that, though I went through such an awful thing, God could use it for good!

I saw Christ as abused . . . maybe not sexually, but He endured an extremely intense contradiction of sinners against Himself, and He experienced rejection, hatred, affliction, malicious intent, and lying. I realized that what I went through only pales in comparison to what He endured at the hands of wicked and perverted humanity.

'Now he that betrayed him gave them a sign, saying, Whomsoever I shall kiss, that same is he: hold him fast. And forthwith he came to Jesus and said, Hail, master; and kissed him.

And Jesus said unto him, Friend, wherefore art thou come? Then came they, and laid hands on Jesus, and took him. (Matthew 26:48-50).

"And when they were come to the place, which is called Calvary, there they crucified him . . .

"Then said Jesus, Father, forgive them; for they know not what they do. And they parted his raiment, and cast lots (Luke 23:33-34).

"He is despised and rejected of men; a man of sorrows, and acquainted with grief: and we hid as it were our faces from him; he was despised, and we esteemed him not. Surely he hath borne our griefs, and carried our sorrows: yet we did esteem him stricken, smitten of God, and afflicted. But he was wounded for

our transgressions, he was bruised for our iniquities: the chastisement of our peace was upon him; and with his stripes we are healed." (Isaiah 53:3-5).

I think now I have a much greater capacity to understand the fellowship of His sufferings, and I know He did all that for me.

Would we think of God at all if life was a bed of roses? The point is that God needs to be glorified and He can be when we call upon Him and He delivers us like only He can.

One day you, like others, will be able to say, "It is good for me that I have been afflicted; that I might learn thy statutes" (Psalm 119:71).

Those powerful words of Job have come to have more precious meaning to me. "Though he slay me, yet will I trust in him . . . " (Job 13:15). I can rejoice, for He has forgiven me! And I can now forgive those that have abused me, and I can serve Him with my whole heart.

As I said, I can live for God only by His grace and through His strength. But I am so thankful that I can! I am a trophy of grace, and thankful for it.

I would encourage anyone who has been abused, even at the hands of a pastor, church leader, or some other minister, to look beyond their abuser and see Christ. As we center our attention on Him and see what He has done for us, we can come to a greater appreciation of true forgiveness and love.

If I can be healed and live for God, then anyone can! To God be the glory!

Debi is truly the survivor of a vicious attack of Satan. He took her, shook her, and tore her, but he could not kill her . . . for she called upon her Savior who came and delivered her from his powerful jaws. The Lord defeated Satan's jaws of death with the weapons of love and forgiveness.

And now Debi is serving our Lord as a Sunday school teacher, speaker, and writer.

Points to Ponder:

Be watchful, even among relatives, and even on church property. Know where your children are at all times, and with whom!

Understand that anyone could be an abuser.

Nothing can replace the watchful care of a loving parent.

If a young person has been abused, expect her or him to deny it at first.

Know that even those who have been abused can obtain the grace of God, through Christ, and still live for Him. In fact, they—*we*—can become trophies of His grace to encourage many others!

The Divorce Dilemma

Divorce strikes every child with a horrific inner death. It is death of an ideal, death of a dream, death of a future. While the parents are dealing with their own fragments, a child must deal with the ruins as well.

Elizabeth was three years old when her parents divorced. Still, she remembers to this day the terrible fights that went on, as though they were emblazoned into her memory. Today, we would never guess that her care-free self ever had to deal with such recollections from so long ago, but they are memories she deals with on a daily basis.

Her mother, Andrea, is a Christian, but Jack, her father, is not. The two world-views and lifestyles clashed horribly, and many times her dad's anger was volcanic. Andrea endured years of abuse before finally fleeing for her safety and sanity. The divorce severed the last connection to the man who hurt her so badly. Or did it?

By the time the dust cleared, there were two little children, Elizabeth and her younger brother, Nathan. Eighteen months her junior, Nathan was indelibly stamped with an inborn love for his dad, and a yearning for his approval.

The divorce agreement declared that the children would spend every other weekend at their dad's house, a large lavish home. Because he had a very good job, he had all the money he wanted and could buy the children all sorts of goodies. In his own way, he was trying to buy their affection.

Meanwhile, he spread a lot of lies about Elizabeth's mother. Since Andrea and Jack knew the same people, it was just another one of his ways to hurt her. She had no idea what to do about it, and prayed, asking the Lord for guidance and wisdom. A godly counselor told her, "Time is a revealer of truth. Just let it go, and ask the Lord to make everything right. In His time, He will." It proved to be one of the best pieces of advice she ever received.

Eventually, Andrea decided that since Jack was their father, they needed to love him. She made it a point not to tear him down in front of them. Elizabeth says, "When we were little, we loved my father and thought the world of him. Only as we got older did we see the difference of his bashing Mom and her *not* bashing him.

Jack's desire to buy his children's affection was a one-sided competition, a rivalry in which their mother didn't participate. Andrea knew that love is not something you buy, it's something you earn. Again, Elizabeth says, "I thought he was great because he gave me everything I wanted. But when I became about 13 or 14, I saw through his desire to buy our love."

In time, each of her parents remarried. Elizabeth and Nathan continued visiting their dad every other weekend, as well as visiting for a few hours on Tuesdays.

There was a vast difference between her mom's and her dad's place. Of course, the homes themselves were very different, with her dad's home being so much nicer than her mom's. There were many other differences as well. At her mom's house, there were rules to follow: chores to do, limits on things like television, movies and computer games, as well as the normal "don't-take-food-into-your-bedrooms" sorts of rules. But at her dad's house, there were no rules at all; everything was free game. It was a child's paradise, a play place in which she could do anything she wanted. Added to the fact that her dad would buy her whatever she desired, it seemed to be a dream come true.

Jack went to all kinds of churches, mostly weak inter-denominational ones where the gospel was a social one, rather than a true gospel of salvation by grace through faith. But during the week, Elizabeth attended her mom's and stepdad's Bible-preaching church, went out on weekly evangelism, and attended youth functions. In the summers, she went to teen camp.

By the time Elizabeth was 14, she was no longer required to visit her dad. Often, however, she chose to go to his house, since she could do anything she wanted! Many times her dad told her, "If you come live with me you can have a TV in your room, and anything you want!" Her mother worried, but said nothing . . . outwardly. On her knees, however, she poured out her soul to her Heavenly Father, "Lord, please work in Elizabeth's heart. Please protect her from the awful influence of her dad, and especially protect her from any abuse. Keep her safe, and please let her one day serve You."

Elizabeth's biweekly visits resulted in coming home with a hateful attitude toward her mom and stepdad. Often it would take days for the bad attitudes to clear out of her heart. Though she had been born-again when she was eleven, the lure of fun and doing whatever she wanted was extremely powerful. It was almost like living on a roller coaster: she would go to her dad's house and do whatever she wanted, then go to her mom's house and get right with God and seek to please God, then go back to her dad's house again.

A huge battle began to rage in Elizabeth's heart. The desire to please herself was great, but she knew what God wanted her to do. It seemed she could hardly bear the thought of giving up her own cravings, but she knew that God was able to give her more than she could ever ask or think. Her dad's house might have been Heaven on earth . . . or was it? There was an instability about her dad's life that bothered her. It wasn't something she could really put her finger on, but it was there nonetheless. It seemed hollow, lacking warmth and love. Her mom's life was so full of love, and so much happier, even though she seemed to have more rules and less "stuff." It was relentless struggle.

Elizabeth said, "I was 16, at youth camp. During the evening service God really spoke to my heart. I surrendered to do anything he wanted me to, even marry a preacher, if that was His will. Lots of conviction led up to my decision. I guess the whole split home thing was very detrimental to me, because I spent every weekend with my dad, and he was absolutely against anything having to do with God. In years gone by, I would make decisions for the Lord at camp (dress standards, etc.) then come home and get made fun of, so I would just leave it behind and forget it. But when I was 16, I just decided that I wanted to serve the Lord myself, no matter what someone else did or said."

It was a monumental decision—a resolution with eternal benefits. Elizabeth eventually stopped visiting her father, instead seeking to serve the Lord with all her heart. God brought a fine young man into her life, a preacher, and now they are married and blessed with three beautiful children. I personally think I have yet to see a happier young couple than Elizabeth and her loving husband, Chris.

I can see several major things in Elizabeth's upbringing that helped her make the right decision. God used the wisdom of the counselor, who showed her mother that "time will tell the truth." Elizabeth's mother chose the high road of not saying bad things about her ex-husband, though she was very tempted and had every opportunity to do so. She realized that to run down her husband to her children would have put them into a terrible position, and they most likely would have sided with the abusive father. The hate needed to stop, and it stopped with her.

Her mother and stepfather's faithfulness to the Lord were also very instrumental in Elizabeth's choice to serve the Lord. She said, "Their lives were centered on the Lord and the church. It brought stability into my life, which I so desperately needed."

Finally, the Word of God did its wonderful work, and the fervent, effectual prayer of a loving mother moved the Hand of God. Elizabeth was under good preaching regularly, and the Lord used His Word to change her heart. And truly, the greatest miracles are miracles of the heart.

****

You've read their stories, and heard how these folks are serving the Lord *in spite* of the things that happened to them in their childhood. Why did I write their stories? Well, two reasons:

- To help parents realize that it is possible, through the grace of God, for our children to turn out right even if we blow it. We all make mistakes, and though many of us do not make errors nearly as blatant as the parents of The Exceptions (at least I hope not!), we can understand that we, too, need the grace of God.

- To help young people realize that they CAN serve God, no matter what their parents have done wrong. If these dear people can surmount the most vile and debilitating traumas, then so can any young person who has human, fallible parents. That includes all of us. We ALL need the grace of God to serve Him.

It's vastly important that we learn from their experiences, so we don't repeat the same mistakes.

CHAPTER 14:
WHAT WILL YOU DO?

"He that knoweth to do good, and doeth it not, to him it is sin" (James 4:17).

*"But be ye doers of the word, and not hearers only, deceiving your own selves"
(James 1:22).*

Patterson got his lions; will you get yours? There are legions of satanic messengers out there in the world, ready to deceive and devour your young people. Stealthy and silent, they are this very moment stalking your home. Will you simply neglect the words of many who have survived, and allow your young people to be taken?

To repeat myself, these principles have been employed by many successful parents, and they have raised godly children who are right now reaching the world for Jesus. These are not man-invented schemes, nor are they ideas that have been ineffective, nor are they philosophies that worked for some other culture at some other time period. They are effective, biblical philosophies that work here and now. It has been proven by dozens of godly generations.

I think many Bible-believing Christians have too long been wondering, deep down, if the Bible way of training and raising children really works. Through these studies, I trust that we have found that, yes, **the Bible way *really is* the best way.** Furthermore, it is the *only* way (except for someone to turn to God from a lost background) to raise a child who will become a godly adult.

****

Tammy, a pastor's wife who's part of a growing congregation, has nine children, most of whom are grown up, serving the Lord in various parts of the country. After church on Sunday, to see her laughing and talking to people as she stands in the foyer next to her husband, we would never guess the heartache and abuse she endured as a child.

Sexually abused by her cousin, beaten by her father, and neglected by her hard-working mother, Tammy had no idea what real love was like until she met someone who pointed her to a loving Savior. It was then that she felt the warm glow of love, the clean feeling of forgiveness, and the serenity of acceptance. It was a brand-new life.

But life is not without scars, and every night she fought another battle with her memories. As children came, she worried about whether or not she could be a real mother, when she had no idea what a real mother was like. Finally, her desperation drove her to her knees, where she begged for the grace of God to give her the wisdom and strength to raise godly children. So urgent was her desire that she almost frantically pored over the Scriptures, seeking truth and receiving both truth and grace.

God, in His great mercy, has blessed her with a group of dedicated, loving children that are now preachers, pastor's wives, or faithful church members that are raising their own little children to love and serve the Lord.

"So, tell me," I commented to Tammy one day after church. "Is there anything you can think of that you did that pointed your children in the direction of serving God?"

She paused for just a moment, obviously unaccustomed to the question. Giving a puzzled expression, she replied, "Well, I don't know. I guess I would say that God did it. I just did what He said in His Word: love them, whoop them, and pray, pray, pray! God did the rest."

I could only smile at her incredible victories, knowing her as I do. I can say that, with God's help, guidance, and strength, she did a tremendous job.

The amazingly beautiful part is the fact that she had so little with which to start.

Folks, if she can do it, so can we. She has an awesome God, and so do we. All it takes is a willing heart, a real faith, and a dedicated life—and we, too, can raise **godly children who are LIONPROOF!**

APPENDIX

Are you Lionproof?

It's wonderful that you as a reader have decided to stand up for your children, and to alter the future of your family. Did you know that the best thing you can do to Lion-proof your children is to be Lionproof yourself? Someone once said, "prayer doesn't change things; prayer changes *you*, and *you change things.*" The principle applied goes like this: as you work and learn and toil and prepare your kids to overcome the Devil and have joyful effective lives now and forever, you will become a stronger parent, and that will pave the way for Lionproof kids.

So I pray you have experienced one of two things in reading this book:

1) You are strengthened your own defenses against Satan—you have become a more committed Christian.
2) You personally are sensing an untold vulnerability. Where others have found fulfillment, you still seem empty.

If #2 rings true, this little section is for you! The purpose of God's Word is to teach and settle each of us in the matters of our soul:

> **To open their eyes, and to turn them from darkness to light, and from the power of Satan unto God, that they may receive forgiveness of sins, and inheritance among them which are sanctified by faith that is in me.**
> **–Acts 26:18**

In this verse, Paul, a first-gen Christian, describes the purpose of his life. And he describes the need in yours.

*   *"To open their eyes"* There is an eyesight beyond your *physical* eyes, in your heart. When we understand what our thoughts and actions really look like to God, our eyes are being *opened*.

Jesus said unto them, If ye were blind, ye should have no sin: but now ye say, We *see; therefore your **sin remaineth**.* John 9:41 Jesus means that if you think you're okay because you're good, you're not. But if you've come to the place where you see how unworthy you are of God's blessing and His heaven, you've begun to see.

- *". . .and to turn them from darkness to light"* When you recognize how wrong you've been before God, not just for what you have done, but for what you are—a sinner—then you will want to turn from all the junk and from the selfish stuff. It's all phony happiness anyway!

- *". . . and from the power of **Satan unto God**"* The Devil prowls about seeking to kill his next victim. If you die without being saved, you will spend eternity with him. He wants you. *"Then shall he (God) say also unto them on the left hand, Depart from me, ye cursed, into everlasting fire, prepared for the devil and his angels:"* Matthew 25:41

A young Army medic was attending our church near Fort Hood, Texas. He was a "pick-yourself-up-by-your-own-bootstraps" kind of guy, and as he attended the services and heard the Bible preached, he began to realize that there was *no way* he would be able to save himself from his own sin. He spoke with the pastor about his condition a few times over a week or so. The progression of emotion went like this:

(Fear) *Hey Pastor, I was running my Army P.T. this morning, and it occurred to me that if that bus ran over me, according to the Bible, I'd go (pointing down) THERE!"*

(Anger) *Pastor, I learned that the Bible is scientifically accurate and God really did create the world; including the dinosaurs, and you and me. The Devil's been lying to me and that makes me mad!*

(Sadness) *Ya know what I understand for the first time, Pastor? I see that I have been kicking sand in the face of the One who died on the cross FOR ME!*

At that point the pastor asked the big soldier is he would like to quit kicking and to instead receive Christ into his heart & life. He did, bravely bowing his head and humbly asking the Lord to forgive him of his sins, and to come into his heart—trusting him completely as his personal Savior. The result?

(Joy) *Ya know what? I feel like a new man! Let's tell the world about Jesus!*

- *". . . that they may receive forgiveness of sins"* Just as the Soldier did, so can you. To escape the deadly claws of your real enemy, turn to your real FRIEND, who is ready to forgive you and come inside you. That's the way to really be "lion-proofed"—from the inside out! Oh, receive him weary soul!

- *". . . and inheritance among them which are sanctified by faith that is in me."* By putting faith and confidence in His work to win your battle, as performed on the cross and certified by His rising again, you can confidently go forward KNOWING that you will make it one day to an inheritance of a home in Heaven prepared for you. Right now— get it settled. Invite Christ to be your Lord and Savior!

> Let not your heart be troubled: ye believe in God, believe also in me. In my Father's house are many mansions: if it were not so, I would have told you. I go to prepare a place for you. And if I go and prepare a place for you, I WILL COME AGAIN, AND RECEIVE YOU UNTO MYSELF; THAT WHERE I AM, THERE YE MAY BE ALSO. And whither I go ye know, and the way ye know . . . I am the way, the truth, and the life: no man cometh unto the Father, but by me.
> —Jesus, in John 14:1-6

BIBLIOGRAPHY

[1]The Barna Group, Ventura CA, September 28, 2011, Six Reasons Young Christians Leave Church; http://www.barna.org/teens-next-gen-articles/528-six-reasons-young-christians-leave-church, Accessed January 2013

[2]The Barna Group, September 11, 2006, Most Twenty=Somethings Put Christianity on the Shelf Following Spiritually Active Teen Years; http://www.barna.org/barna-update/article/16-teensnext-gen/147-most-twentysomethings-put-christianity-on-the-shelf-following-spiritually-active-teen-years, accessed May 2012

[3]Tse, Rhoda, The Christian Post, Washington D.C., January 12, 2006, US Church Leaders, Youth Ministers Address Chgristian Youth Fallout, http://www.christianpost.com/news/u-s-church-leaders-youth-ministers-address-christian-youth-fallout-13940/, Accessed 2011

[4]The Barna Group, Ventura CA, February 28, 2005, Parents Describe How They Raise Their Children, http://www.barna.org/barna-update/article/5-barna-update/184-parents-describe-how-they-raise-their-children, Accessed 2012

[5]Kobernat, Joanna Brown (2010 April).*Christian Womanhood.*

[6]Brandon, Dr. Richard and others. *Family Matters: Mental Health of Children and Parents,* Seattle: Human Services Policy Center, Evans School of Public Affairs, University of Washington, 2003

[7]Nauert, Dr. Rick. March 7, 2007;*Family Stress Affects Kids' Physical Health,*http://psychcentral.com/news/2007/03/07/family-stress-affects-kids-physical-health/669.html, Accessed March 2013

[8]Hare, Heather and others. March , 2007; *Children Under Stress Develop More Fevers,*http://www.urmc.rochester.edu/news/story/index.cfm?id=1396 Accessed March 2013

[9]Selvera, Richard and others. February 2008; *Houston Corps of Cadets Fact Sheet.*http://www.class.uh.edu/rotc/corpsofcadets/_docs/HCoC_FactSheet.pdfAccessed March 2013

[10]Green, Don and others. 1999. He's Everything He Claims to Be, and More! Revival Fires Publishing: Claysburg, PA (– his six adult children are serving the Lord full-time to this day)

[11]Parker-Pope, Tara. October 2007; *Marital Spats, Taken to Heart.* New York Times http://www.nytimes.com/2007/10/02/health/02well.html Accessed April 2013

[12]Malens, Joseph. *A Fence or an Ambulance.*http://www.wealthandwant.com/docs/Malins_ambulance.html Accessed April 2013

[13]Spurgeon, Charles H. July 1908; *The Church in Your House.* Sermon preached at Metropolitan Baptist Tabernacle, Newington. http://www.spurgeongems.org/vols52-54/chs3103.pdf. Accessed April 2013

[14]Ray, Dr. Brian. Home Educated and Now Adults.2004. National Home Education Research Institute, Salem, OR

[15]Schmidt, Dr. Marie Evans and others. January 2005; *The Effects of Electronic Media on Children Ages Zero to Six: A History of Research,* The Children's Hospital, Boston, The Kaiser Family Foundation, http://www.kff.org/entmedia/upload/the-effects-of-electronic-media-on-children-ages-zero-to-six-a-history-of-research-issue-brief.pdf, Accessed April 2013

[16]Shute, Nancy. March 2010;*3 Ways Electronic Media Harm Kids' Health and 3 Ways They Can Help,* US News, http://health.usnews.com/health-news/blogs/on-parenting/2010/03/01/3-ways-electronic-media-harm-kids-health-and-3-ways-they-can-help, Accessed April 2013

[17]The Barna Group, February 28, 2005, Parents Describe How They Raise Their Children

[18]Barrett, Laura and others. October 2002, *Study Offers Parents New Insights into When and Why Teens Choose Drinking, Drugs, and Sex,* http://www.sadd.org/teenstoday/study.htm, Boston, Accessed April 2013

[19]Gentile, Douglas A. and others. 2003, Media Violence and Children, Greenwood Publishing Group, Westport, Connecticut

[20] Wertz, Marianna. February 1998, *Why Classical Music is Key to Education,* http://www.schillerinstitute.org/programs/program_symp_2_7_98_tchor_.html#Conclusions. The Schiller Institute, Washington D.C. Accessed April 2013

[21]Gentile, Douglas A..and others. October 2003. *The Effects of Violent Music on Children and Adults,*http://www.psychology.iastate.edu/~dgentile/106027_08.pdf, Accessed April 2013

[22]Gardener, David, *Discipline, Mummy-Bear Style,* March 2012, www.dailymail.co.uk, London, Accessed April 2013

[23]Sir Winston Churchill, *1941, Speech at Harrow School,* http://www.quotationspage.com/quote/27170.html, Accessed April 2013

[24]See the video here: www.huffingtonpost.com/2010/09/13/sixstory-building-collaps_n_715277.html

[25]North Carolina State University Cooperative Extension, *Raising Children: Setting Boundaries,* http://jackson.ces.ncsu.edu/content/RaisingChildren:SettingBoundaries, Accessed April 2013

[26]No author cited. July 2010, *Parents Give Mixed Messages to Teens on Drugs and Alcohol,* http://www.caron.org/parents-give-mixed-messages-to-teens-on-drinking-alcohol.html Caron Treatment Centers, Philadelphia PA Accessed April 2013

[27]No author cited. July 2010, *Improve Communication with Your Kids,* http://earlyinterventionteam.org/wp-content/uploads/2010/07/Improve-Communication-with-Your-Kids.pdf, Accessed April 2013

[28] No author cited. September 2009, *Positive Parenting Can Have Lasting Impact for Generations,* http://oregonstate.edu/ua/ncs/archives/2009/sep/positive-parenting-can-have-lasting-impact-generations. Oregon State University, Accessed April 2013

[29]Lansky, Vicky. 2004, Trouble-Free Travel with Children, Book Peddlers, Minnetonka, MN

[31] No author cited. 2012 *Statistics in the Ministry,*
http://www.pastoralcareinc.com/statistics/, Accessed April 2013

[32] Barrow, Becky. July 2006, *19 Minutes – How Long Working Parents Give Their Children*, http://www.dailymail.co.uk/news/article-396609/19-minutes--long-working-parents-children.html, Accessed April 2013

[33] Small, Dr. Gary. 2009, *Is Technology Fracturing Your Family?*http://www.psychologytoday.com/blog/brain-bootcamp/200906/is-technology-fracturing-your-family, Accessed April 2013

[34] Math 3 (3rd Ed), 2009, BJU Press, Greenville SC

[35] McCurdy, Harold. November, 1957 *The Childhood Pattern of Genius*, http://dc.lib.unc.edu/cgi-bin/showfile.exe?CISOROOT=/jncas&CISOPTR=2278, Accessed April 2013

[36] Ibid

[37] No author cited, September 2007, *Samuel and Nancy Elliot Edison*, http://www.nps.gov/edis/historyculture/samuel-and-nancy-elliott-edison.htm, Accessed April 2013

[38] Schmidt, Cary. July 2007, *Top 15 Questions Christian Teens Ask*,http://caryschmidt.com/2009/07/top-15-questions-christian-teens-ask/, Accessed April 2013

Don't just take a journey...take a COURAGEOUS journey"

The Courageous Journey Network

Eagle Heights Publications

PO Box 443

Raeford, NC 28376

THE UMBRELLA STORY, by Lisa B. Raub,
illustrated by Yuriy Yeremenko

God has established the authorities in our lives to be a continual guide, help, and protection to us as we live on this earth. I think of them as our Umbrella of Protection. As we submit ourselves to our authorities, we are protected from many of Satan's fiery darts, but if we go out from under our Umbrella of Protection, we become exposed to many dangers. Those who have learned this principle find safety and guidance as they stay under the powers that be, which are ordained of God.

Sometimes, however, we learn that our authorities are not perfect. This is like a hole in our umbrella, allowing danger in our lives. How can we patch up the hole? Why does it seem to take so long for God to fix the problem? This parable will help all ages to understand the answers. Paperback, for all ages.

Price: $6.75 + $3.99 shipping

Order from Eagle Heights Publications by going on
www.thecourageousjourney.com

Bulk copies available for a discount

Bulk copies of <u>Lionproof: Keeping Your Children from the Claws of the Devil</u> are available by contacting Eagle Heights Publications—eagleheightspiblications@gmail.com., or writing the above address.